MERV *On Talk Shows*

"They used to call talk show hosts traffic cops, but it's not all that easy. You have to put a framework around your guests . . . lead them in the right direction. There's just one thing you can't have when you step out there, and that's fear."

●

"Politicians are very hard to interview unless you throw them a surprise question—but they've been tossed every question known to man!"

●

"Athletes are pretty good, but raw and undisciplined."

●

"American actresses tend to be too leery; they hold back. But foreign girls are great—Sophia Loren, Lollobrigida, Cardinale—they're all fine talkers with a gift for candor."

●

"Most singers are dull and have no sense of humor about themselves—except for Bob Goulet who can be very funny . . . ."

MERV

Michael B. Druxman

LEISURE BOOKS ✿ NEW YORK CITY

A LEISURE BOOK

Published by

Nordon Publications, Inc.
Two Park Avenue
New York, N.Y. 10016

About the Author

Michael B. Druxman was born in Seattle, Washington, and graduated from the University of Washington with a major in sociology. His avid interest in motion pictures and the theater stems from early childhood. As he grew older, he became active in Seattle's community theater movement and eventually formed his own group, Actors' Theater.

Moving to Los Angeles in 1963, Mr. Druxman produced and directed a film, *Genesis*. In 1966, he formed his own public relations firm, which caters to both show business and commercial clients.

He has contributed to *Films in Review*, as well as *Coronet*, for which he wrote a regular feature, "Yesterday at the Movies." He is the author of biographies on Paul Muni and Basil Rathbone, as well as the highly acclaimed *Make It Again, Sam: A Survey of Movie Remakes* and *One Good Film Deserves Another: A Survey of Movie Sequels*. His most recent work is *The Musical: From Broadway to Hollywood*.

Mr. Druxman resides in Calabasas, California.

Acknowledgments

Biographies of this type would be impossible to write without the assistance of many individuals. I would, therefore, like to thank Joan Crosby, Al Drebin, Don Freeman, June C. Malkemus, Doug McClelland, Bill Meyer, and James Robert Parish for their help in securing research materials for my use; the family, friends, and associates of Merv Griffin for sharing their experiences, knowledge, and opinions with me; and, particularly, Dick Kleiner for recommending me for this assignment.

Finally, a special note of thanks to Merv, himself, who both graciously and candidly opened the doors of his life to me, making what is often hard work, fun.

Prologue

Richard Castellano is the first to arrive at the Hollywood Palace Theater on Vine Street. The well-fed star of *Lovers and Other Strangers* and *The Godfather* doesn't want to miss the debut of his new CBS-TV series, "Joe and Sons" and, since its air time is eight-thirty, he's decided it's best to watch it here, lest he be late for his appearance on "The Merv Griffin Show."

Castellano, who is accompanied by twenty-one-year-old daughter Margaret and his personal publicist, explains to the program's make-up man that he "never uses the stuff," then, with entourage in tow, is ushered down the long, bleak hallway to the green room. This functionally furnished gathering place, full of anxious guests waiting to be called before the television cameras, is located in the basement of the building, directly underneath the stage.

The young production assistant switches the television set at the end of the room to the CBS network, tells the trio that the bar will be open in a few minutes and departs to await the arrival of the next guest. Also scheduled for the show this evening are Don Adams, Lynn Redgrave, and Henny Youngman.

Doffing the jacket of his blue pin-stripe suit, Castellano sits down on one of the room's three sofas and turns to his press representative. "The first time I did Merv's show," he muses, "was in New York—right after *Lovers and Other Strangers* came out. I was home doing some plastering when I got this call from somebody on the production staff, asking me to come over to the theater and appear on the program—in forty-five minutes.

"I tried to explain that I was in work clothes—covered with plaster—but they didn't care. Two guests had cancelled out and they needed somebody *fast*.

"Well, I dropped what I was doing, washed up a bit, jumped into my car and broke all speed records getting from my home in Woodside over to the theater, just off Times Square. I even ran the last block because I had trouble parking.

"Within two minutes after I walked through the stage door—sweaty and out of breath—I was in front of the cameras."

"How did Merv react to your . . . attire?" asks the publicist.

"He made me feel like I was wearing a tuxedo. We'd never met before and all he really knew about me was in a two page studio bio—yet we improvised for more than a half hour. It was completely spontaneous, but he knew what he was doing every minute of the time."

The green room is suddenly invaded by a mob of about eight "civilians" (people not in show business), family and friends of Henny Youngman. The violin-packing comedian is in Hollywood for a couple of days to do a cameo bit in a film, so it's only natural that his manager would book him on Merv's show.

Youngman, a large man, enters, gives his rooting section a cursory greeting, then tells them, "I want you to sit out in the audience. That's where I'm going to need the laughs."

After the group departs, the comic spots Castellano and goes over to introduce himself and his heavy-set grandson, a lad in his twenties who has remained with him to lend support. Castellano, a long-time admirer of

10

Youngman, trades compliments with the older man and chuckles at jokes until the production assistant invites Henny to be made-up.

It's eight-thirty, a half hour before taping begins on the stage upstairs. Just as the opening credits of Castellano's "Joe and Sons" appear on the television screen, the assistant returns, unlocks a door leading to a small kitchen, and asks if anybody would like some liquid refreshment. It's not a drinking crowd tonight and the young man only receives requests for Cokes and 7-Ups.

The half-dozen occupants of the green room seem to enjoy the debuting comedy series which has Castellano playing a widower from New Jersey who is raising his two sons. (The program was cancelled in January 1976.) Amid their laughter, the third guest of the evening, Don Adams, makes his appearance with an attractive young lady clutching his arm. Unlike the two other celebrities who are wearing jackets and ties, the former star of "Get Smart" is garbed in a leisure suit. He chooses not to watch the television show and leads his brunette friend out into the hallway where they lean against the wall, talking softly to each other.

A bit harried, the production assistant is back in the kitchen a few minutes later to prepare some drinks for actress Lynn Redgrave and her several companions. The daughter of Britian's Sir Michael Redgrave has decided to await her entrance in a private dressing room just off the stage.

The players are all present now. Their faces may be different from the other personalities who will appear on one of the remaining four segments of the program to tape this week, but their purposes for being there, and their actions prior to showtime, do not vary significantly. Occasionally, a guest might have one drink too many in order to bolster his courage before appearing in front of the cameras. The prospect of being *oneself* on a show that will be seen by millions of Americans is certainly enough to unnerve anybody. Otherwise, the procedure is pretty much the same, night after night.

Every guest on the ninety-minute program—no matter who he or she is—receives the same salary—AFTRA (American Federation of Television/Radio Artists) scale, which totals $337.50.

Why does such high-priced talent appear for such a pittance?

There are two basic reasons—exposure and plugs.

A variety performer, for example, will find that the demand for his services in nightclubs, concerts, and the like will increase in relationship to his television exposure. The better known he is, the more the public is willing to shell out their hard-earned dollars to see him when he appears in their particular town or when they travel to a resort like Las Vegas, Lake Tahoe or Miami. The same theory holds for actors and actresses who spend part of their working time doing summer stock or dinner theaters. There certainly seems to be a correlation between offers and salaries from these regional theaters, and the number of times a star has appeared on the tube during the previous few months.

If a guest wants to give a nationwide plug to his new movie, television show, book, or stage productions, what better place than on "The Merv Griffin Show"?

Yes, there definitely are factors that more than compensate for the artists' minimal fee for this program.

Nine P.M. In the green room, Castellano receives congratulations for his series. Somebody switches the set to the closed circuit channel and, a moment or two later, music from Mort Lindsey's orchestra signals that it's showtime.

Brown-haired, blue-eyed, five-foot-ten-inch Merv Griffin makes his entrance to a warm welcome from his studio audience. In his fiftieth year, the beloved talk show host is looking trimmer than he has in some time. As opposed to his guests waiting in the room below, Merv is totally relaxed. He has done this show five times a week for many years and, although he is never quite sure what surprises a particular program might hold in store for him, his long experience has made him secure enough to know that he can handle any situation which might develop.

He greets the house and, especially, the small, venerable Miss Miller, his most ardent fan who seldom misses a show. In days past, this steadfast supporter had regularly graced the audiences of both the Steve Allen and Jack Paar "Tonight" programs, but, for the last few years, her affections have belonged to Merv.

Following a few casual remarks and a listing of the evening's guests, the host moves to the orchestra, grabs a hand mike and begins trading quips with first trumpeter Jack Sheldon, a semi-regular on the program who sometimes moonlights as an actor. Sheldon leaves his station with the musicians, joining Merv on the stage floor for a duet. Despite the vast difference in the men's singing styles, the performance is an entertaining one, and is followed by a commercial break.

Down in the green room, the production assistant summons Adams to the stage. The self-assured comic actor smiles at his lady friend, who blows him a kiss, then ascends the steel steps to await his introduction.

Adams is a good guest, responding immediately to Merv's well-directed questions. The possessor of a wealth of anecdotes, Adams puts the show's star, as well as the audience, into near hysterics with a story dealing with acid-tongued comedian Don Rickles and actor Joey Forman.

Merv keeps Don on alone for nearly twenty minutes and, during this time, the funnyman talks about "Don Adams' Screen Test," his new syndicated television show, the plugging of which is, of course, the primary motivation for his visit to Vine Street. From a series of film clips Adams has with him, one can see that the program's premise is fully explained by the title. Amateur actors perform with pros to recreate scenes from classic motion pictures, and as Adams puts it, "the out-takes are the funniest things about the show."

Coming out of a commercial break at the program's halfway point, Merv introduces Richard Castellano, who strides on stage while the orchestra plays the main theme from *The Godfather*. He shakes hands with his host, then Adams, finally sitting to Merv's left.

Castellano discusses his new series, the problems of living in Los Angeles (his show was taped there) on a temporary basis when "home" is in New Jersey and, after another break for commercials, explains the involved method he uses to formulate his on-screen and stage characterizations. Merv appears keenly interested in this dissertation, which prompts Adams to relate a story of his experience in the 1962 Broadway play, *Harold*. The anecdote illustrates the point that it takes much hard work and study to develop the detailed performances upon which actors such as Castellano have built their reputations.

Watching the show on the set in the green room, a slightly disgruntled Henny Youngman looks at his watch, noting that the program is already into its final half hour. He is to be the final guest on the bill tonight. "They sure aren't leaving much time for me," he remarks to anyone who might be listening.

Lynn Redgrave, in Los Angeles to appear in a play at the Huntingdon Hartford Theater, is brought out next. Downstairs, Castellano's publicist comments on how

14

attractive the actress looks since she's slimmed down. There's absolutely no resemblance between the woman on the stage above and the overweight star of *Georgy Girl*.

The English actress talks about her impressions of America, then corrects Adams when he says that her father, Sir Michael Redgrave, *was* one of the world's greatest actors and *was* one of his idols. "He's still alive," she snaps.

Finally, with ten minutes left in the show, Youngman is introduced. Instead of sitting with Merv and the other guests, he, as previously arranged, moves center stage and—violin in hand—proceeds to do a few minutes of his well-worn material. The audience is not very receptive.

A final breakaway for a commercial and, when the program resumes, there is only enough time for Merv to bid a general good-bye to his guests and viewers. The production credits move swiftly up the screen to the playing of Mort Lindsey's orchestra, their music ceasing the moment the television monitor fades to black. The show is over.

Merv takes time to thank each of his guests for appearing on the program and invites them to return. Then he hurries offstage to his private and well-shielded dressing room to change from his suit into more casual street attire.

After some quick "Good-byes" and "It was funs" between themselves, the guests quickly head for the stage door and out into the midst of a dozen or more autograph seekers. The celebrities stop for a moment to sign a book or two, then look toward the theater ushers for aid in making their escapes.

Only Castellano and his companions linger in the darkened backstage area tonight. He has not seen Merv since the latter moved to Los Angeles in 1970 and he wants this brief reunion to be more than just a meeting in front of the watchful eye of the camera.

Griffin keeps him waiting only a minute. Emerging from his dressing room with briefcase in hand, it is obvious that Merv has an appointment to keep, but he takes a few moments to chat with his acquaintance from the Big Apple and to meet his daughter, Margaret. Castellano's account of his initial and almost impromptu appearance on the show brings forth a chuckle from Griffin, who then announces that he must leave. They embrace warmly—as old friends sometimes do—and Merv disappears through the stage door, cutting across the parking lot to avoid the autograph hounds who are being kept in check by the ushers. Usually he enjoys meeting his fans, but tonight he's in a hurry.

As Castellano and company follow the host into the alley, the actor comments to his publicist, "You know, he's a very nice man."

During the past decade, Merv Griffin has been described by television critics as a "hip choir boy," a "sophisticated wit," "the total man," and "the perennial boy-next-door." Yet, despite these tags by a host of the nation's top video journalists, it is perhaps the words of Richard Castellano which most aptly describe both the public and private image of this veteran of the talk show wars: "He's a very nice man."

Merv's soft-spoken ways, regrettably, were not sufficient to win him the crown of "talk show king" when he did battle on CBS-TV in 1969-72 against the urbane humor of Johnny Carson of NBC and ABC's Joey Bishop, who was later replaced by Dick Cavett. Except for rare occasions when Carson was on vacation, Merv ran a consistent second to "The Tonight Show" host and, after two and a half years, threw in the towel,

16

leaving the network to return to the market in which he achieved his initial success—syndicated television.

Not surprisingly, there is a rather large segment of the population who much prefer Merv's program to that of the man who defeated him. They argue that whereas Carson is quick-witted and always in control, he is also insensitive to people, often taking unfair advantage of a not-so-clever guest. Merv, on the other hand, is a listener who is genuinely interested in what his guests have to say. If somebody is nervous or stumbles, Griffin has that deft ability to put the individual at ease.

According to pudgy comedian Jackie Vernon, who has done the program innumerable times, "Merv knows just how to top you to get a funny response."

So why did Griffin only "place" in the network race?

Experts claim Carson was so well established with late night viewers, it would have been absolutely impossible for *anybody* to steal a significant portion of his audience from him. "Nice guys" don't always finish first.

Today, a busy Merv Griffin is satisfied to be away from the network rat race. Aside from his highly successful talk program for Metromedia, the multimillionaire produces television game shows, has a couple of pilot projects in the works, and owns seven radio stations on the East Coast, as well as a tape/film company, an air charter service, a mail order firm, and a building in New York City.

Deluged with many business decisions daily, Griffin admits, "Frankly, I'm more comfortable doing the show than I am walking about in life. It's relaxing and gets me away from phones ringing all the time."

A miniature empire like his does not spring up overnight, however. Indeed, there were many times during Griffin's show business career when it was doubtful whether the performer, despite his stout

17

ambition, would ever reach a place of distinction.

Part of his problem was bad timing. His career as a band singer was ill-fated because, when he entered the field, the big dance band craze had begun its irreversible decline; he was under contract to a major motion picture studio during a period when Hollywood was in one of its worst depressions; and his later chores as a television emcee and quiz master did not elevate him above others in the field who were doing like jobs.

It was almost an accident, a quirk of fate, which enabled this scion of a middle-class California family to prove to the world and himself what he could do best. After nearly two decades of struggling *against* the current, he seized upon this new-found opportunity, and developed his career—surmounting the harsh toll on his personal life—to the sometimes lonely zenith where it is today.

This is the story of Merv Griffin's untiring and, ultimately, rewarding struggle for recognition and identity; of his friendships and feuds with the famous in the varied and often treacherous world of entertainment.

One

July 6, 1925 was not a red letter day in the annals of San Mateo, California, nor was the date a very memorable one for the nation as a whole.

Residents of this small, sophisticated community —located on San Francisco Bay, about twenty miles south of the fabulous metropolis itself —picked up their copies of the *San Mateo Times* that Monday evening to read about William Jennings Bryan and how he had just arrived in Dayton, Tennessee, to prepare his landmark case against John T. Scopes, the teacher who'd dared to lecture his pupils on Darwin's theory of evolution. Up in Boston, authorities were still recovering bodies from the tragic Dreyfus Hotel fire, which had claimed forty-three lives.

There were even more unfortunate, if historically unimportant, events occurring closer to home. In nearby Hillsborough, Federal narcotics agents busted a Chinese dope smuggling ring; other government officials closed down road houses that were violating prohibition laws; and, over the weekend, two people were killed in automobile accidents, and another person drowned at Brighton Beach.

While the good citizens of San Mateo were reading of these calamities, Mrs. Rita Robinson Griffin was in Mills Memorial Hospital giving birth to her second child. The infant was a male and he was to be christened Mervyn Edward Griffin, Jr.

Rita Robinson, the daughter of a newspaperman, had met her future husband, Mervyn Edward Griffin, Sr., in a bank where both were employed. Each was a native of the San Francisco area and a good Irish Catholic. Indeed, the Griffin family, which had picked up a bit of Welsh blood over the years, originally came from County Clare in Ireland.

Mervyn, Senior, was one of five brothers, affectionately known to their friends as "the Griffin boys with their lace curtain names." The other siblings' monikers were Clarence (alias "Peck"), Milton, Elmer, and Frank. Milton worked for an ice company, Frank was a salesman for a paper manufacturer, and Mervyn, Peck, and Elmer were tennis champions.

Peck Griffin won the U.S. doubles championship three times and brother Mervyn captured both the Pacific Coast and California State singles titles. However, it was the unusual feats of Elmer that attracted the attention of Ripley's *Believe It or Not* on three separate occasions.

The first write-up told of how he played and defeated champion tennis star "Little Bill" Johnson *without* using a racket. When Johnson hit the ball to him, Elmer would catch it and *throw* it back. The final score was 6-1.

Next, Ripley reported how Griffin had won three Oregon State tennis titles in one afternoon, and, finally, there was the story of the match in which Elmer wore roller skates, emerging victorious over his opponent, who wore sneakers.

When twenty-one-year-old Mervyn Griffin married Rita Robinson in 1922, he decided to forsake the financially uncertain life of the tennis circuit and teach others the sport at which he was so proficient. He became a tennis pro, working, as time went by, at such places as the Dominican Convent in San Raphael, San Mateo's Peninsula Golf and Country Club, the Burlingame Country Club, the Crocker Estate, and the George Cameron Estate.

The newlyweds purchased a little house on San Mateo's modest 5th Avenue. The first child, a daughter, was christened Barbara, and she was joined two years later by Mervyn, Jr., who, to avoid the inevitable confusion with his namesake, was nicknamed Buddy by his mother.

Merv remembers his childhood as being "happy and secure." He lived in a close-knit, loving household. When there were family problems, neither he nor his sister was burdened with them. It was a healthy atmosphere, one that allowed him to learn his true worth as a person.

"Every Sunday," he recalls, "there would be twenty or thirty people over for dinner—friends, relatives, tennis chums of my Dad. After supper, everybody would gather 'round the piano and sing song after song."

Mervyn, Senior, according to his son, was a "total sports enthusiast," who had a marvelous sense of humor and a tendency toward playing practical jokes. "We never had a close father-son relationship—the type where just the two of us would go hunting or fishing—but he was fun to be around and always made me laugh. Outwardly, he may not have been a very affectionate man, but there was never any question that he loved me and was very proud of what I did."

One of his father's occasional tenins opponents was Bishop Fulton J. Sheen, who would always call the senior Griffin when he was in the San Francisco area, so they could play a match together. On one visit, the clergyman phoned the Griffin household and the call was answered by his friend's sister-in-law, Helen Parsell. Thinking that somebody was pulling her leg, Mrs. Parsell said: "Well, Bishop, *this* is Pope Pius the Tenth."

With that, she hung up, and, to say the least, was

21

more than a little embarrassed when she learned later that she had, indeed, been talking with the famous religious leader.

Rita Griffin was a witty, warm and independent woman, who gave her time (and still does) to charities and people in need. Says her son: "She wasn't a clinging kind of mother, but let Barbara and me develop naturally in our own directions."

Young Merv was four when the Great Depression hit. "We didn't fare too badly," he remembers. "There was still plenty of food on the table, but Dad, who was working in a sporting goods shop then, was unable to keep up the payments on our house. For a time, we moved in with my grandmother."

It was at this early point in his life that Merv began taking piano lessons. Claudia Robinson, his aunt, taught the boy who could then hardly reach the keyboard. "He was so little," she recalled later. "He had to play standing up. I loved him. He was just a doll. So little. So talented."

After Aunt Claudia had taught her nephew everything she knew about the piano, she and Rita decided that the enthusiastic Buddy should get more advanced training from a San Francisco instructor. Rita paid for these sessions out of her grocery money, since it had been decided that Mervyn, Senior, would not be informed of his son's lessons. The ladies feared that, to the sports-minded elder Griffin, a piano-playing son might be considered a sissy.

Merv was fourteen before his father learned how skillful he had become at the keyboard. The occasion was Mervyn, Senior's, birthday party, a large affair attended by family and friends.

"I did so enjoy hearing young Mervyn at his recital," said a neighbor to the somewhat bewildered father. "He played the Greig concerto beautifully."

22

His father, seeking clarification, called him over. "Buddy," he asked in a noncommittal tone, "do you play the piano?"

"Yes, Dad," was the uncertain reply.

To the youth, it seemed like hours went by as he watched his father ponder this startling new revelation. Then Griffin said in his matter-of-fact manner, "Well, get over to the piano and let's hear you play."

This was, perhaps, the most important performance in the future star's life. He sat at the keyboard for two solid hours, with his father right beside him enjoying every minute of it. When Merv finished a piece, he was told; "Play something else."

From that point on, Mervyn, Jr., had the permanent job as accompanist at the Griffin household's Sunday sing-alongs.

"One thing about my Dad," says Merv, "he never pushed me into sports. I played some tennis, but he never expected me to follow in his footsteps."

Merv was well on his way to becoming a classical concert pianist when he discovered popular music. He was at the house of a friend and, while looking through some sheet music, came across "In a Little Gypsy Tearoom."

Merv remembers: "I started playing with the tune . . . improvising along the way . . . and became absolutely fascinated with the freedom inherent in this kind of music. That was the end of my classical career."

As a child, Merv was already starting to perform. He'd stage shows and organize circuses. Family clothing was snatched from closets to costume actors; all the bedspreads were out on the lawn for tents; and cages were built to house the neighborhood animals. On other occasions, revival meeting were held in the backyard, with all the kids singing at the top of their lungs.

"I guess I was inspired by those Mickey Rooney and

Judy Garland movies," Merv muses. "I'd put on a show anywhere."

When Merv was eight, he decided to become a newspaper editor and founded the *Whispering Winds*, a sheet that reported on various neighborhood events. Unfortunately, the publication, which was printed on an early version of the Ditto machine, did not have a long life. Recalls Rita: "One day he printed that the next-door neighbors had a fight. One subscription was cancelled. Then he printed a joke he didn't understand—and *everybody* cancelled."

Merv's favorite movie star was none other than dashing Errol Flynn and, when he was sixteen years old, he got the opportunity to meet the screen's Captain Blood in person. Flynn was a good friend of Uncle Elmer, who, in 1936, had founded the West Side Tennis Club (now the Standard Club) in Los Angeles. It catered almost exclusively to people in the film industry. Whenever Errol was between marriages, he would board with Elmer, who, like the swashbuckler, also had a reputation for being a "rounder."

On this particular summer vacation, naive young Merv was invited to spend some time with his colorful uncle in Los Angeles. Arriving at the bachelor quarters, he was shocked to see "Robin Hood" standing in the living room—stark naked.

"I was dumbfounded," he recalls. "I didn't know what to say. Here was my idol—(I'd seen all his pictures)—and the first time I met him, he was in the raw with a drink in his hand.

"But what really threw me is when these beautiful ladies would come over and he *still* wouldn't put any clothes on."

A few days after he'd arrived at Uncle Elmer's, Merv received a call from his mother, who wanted to know if he was enjoying himself.

"I'm having a lot of fun, Mom," he gushed, "and guess what! Errol Flynn is staying with us!"

There was a brief silence at the other end of the line, followed by a very quiet, but firm, "Let me speak to your uncle."

Elmer took the phone and proceeded to calm his sister-in-law with lines like, "Don't worry, Rita," and "the boy's fine." Then, Merv got on the wire again, capping the conversation with, "Everything's great, Mom. They send me to the movies every day."

Merv had one major problem during his youth. He liked to eat, and eat, and eat. In short, he was fat.

"My whole family was fat," he claims. "Everyone at home—Mom, Dad, Barbara—was constantly on a diet."

Children, of course, can be very cruel and Merv well remembers the harsh chant of his classmates, "Fat, fat, the water rat!"

His first eight years of education were at St. Matthew's, a parochial school that employed strict discipline. Then, Merv transferred to San Mateo High, where he developed a defense mechanism that enabled him to cope with the hurt that was synonymous with his large physical stature. He became the class clown.

"I did it to gain the acceptance of my classmates," he admits.

Alice Motto (now Mrs. Alice Underwood), who attended an orchestra class with Merv, recalls him as an amiable, but heavy kid—definitely not handsome—with pudgy little hands. "He was always causing a disturbance," she says. "Mr. Dunn, the instructor, would constantly be saying, 'Mervyn, please quiet down, now.' "

One of the youth's favorite pranks was sticking his bass fiddle (the instrument he played in class) out the window and plunking the strings. The sound would echo throughout the school's courtyard, disturbing all of the classes that were in session.

An elderly algebra teacher at St. Matthew's ("she must have been one hundred years old," remembers Merv) who'd flunked Merv in that course, would invariably react to the unscheduled concerts with: "There's that funny little fat boy again."

"There was another time," laughs Merv, "that Mom had to almost bring me home in a barrel. I'd played a trick on this girl and she was chasing me around the classroom when my pants caught on a desk, practically ripping them off. Was I embarrassed!"

The more relaxed academic atmosphere of San Mateo High had an effect on Merv's initial report card, which boasted three Fs and a D. "I was a terrible student. Had a C average all through school. Luckily, however, my folks weren't pressure parents. Certainly, they were disappointed in my grades, but there were never any severe punishments. If I was going to do better work, we all knew that *I* had to do it on my own, and that they couldn't force that choice on me.

"I never really liked school. Frankly, the most valuable education I've had has been on the talk show."

Despite his overabundance of pounds, Merv's leprechaun personality made him quite popular at San Mateo, particularly with the girls, who enjoyed his funny sense of humor and the fact that he played the piano. Yet, *he* was still bothered by his size, so, on the night of the Junior Prom, he tried to do something about the problem.

"I was in love with a girl named Ethel," he remembers. "I looked in the mirror and said, 'I can't let her see me this heavy,' so I went into my father's closet and took out every belt I could find—ten of them—and strapped myself up.

"It didn't work, though. There were ripples all over

26

me and I looked like an accordion. The whole incident was really rather sad."

Merv's zest for fun was not confined to the hours he spent in school. At home, he regularly sneaked into his older sister's room while she was out and read the latest entries in her secret diary. Then, at dinner, he would "innocently" ask the young girl such pointed questions as, "Have you been to the lumberyard lately, Barbara? Did you meet any new boys there?"

It didn't take long for big sister to realize that bratty brother had been reading her very private thoughts. She'd scream her frustration to her mother, while Merv tried to control his hysterical laughter.

Merv's closest friends in school were Bob Murphy, now the producer of his talk show, and the future jazz artist Cal Tjader. Like Merv, Murphy was also interested in music—the drums. "I couldn't play worth a damn," he says, "but I had the best looking set of Slingerland drums around San Francisco. In fact, Cal Tjader had a terrible looking drum set. Then he saw mine and flipped. Of course, you know what happened. He learned to play drums on *my* set."

Regarding Merv, Murphy recalls that "he liked people and took the time to get to know them. He had a lot of friends at San Mateo High."

Bob, Cal, and Merv's other school pals were always welcome at the Griffin home, located at 705 South Eldorado. (Mervyn, Senior, and Rita had moved into this modestly-priced residence with Grandmother and Aunts during the Depression.) Indeed, friends of both offspring were included in family outings and even vacations at places like Yosemite or Sonora.

Merv: "It wasn't unusual for us to bring three or four friends on trips with us—all piled into the back of a station wagon. Our vacations were *always* fun."

When Merv got his driver's license at age sixteen, his

father, like most parents, was a bit hesitant to let his son drive the family station wagon, especially since it was a new one. But, one day, the boy accompanied his father to the country club and the senior Griffin, knowing Merv was a responsible lad, turned the keys over to him with instructions to *drive carefully*.

Immediately, the youth picked up some friends (including Cal), and took them for a ride. It was only natural that this inexperienced driver would want to test the vehicle's handling capabilities *off* the road . . . which is how the wagon just happened to wind up in a creek.

Responding to Merv's urgent phone call, his father arrived with some chums, who aided him in rescuing the automobile.

"You'll never drive this car again," said his furious father, as they headed back to the club in the muddied vehicle. However, upon their arrival, he realized that his son needed transportation home, so, once again, he gave Merv the keys.

A few weeks later, his father let Merv take the car out one evening, but gave him firm orders not to go into San Francisco where the streets would be filled with traffic.

"An hour or so later," recalls Merv, "I was in San Francisco, speeding down Market Street with a couple of friends. I stopped for a light, when who should cross the street in front of the car, but my Dad. He looked right at me, yet didn't do a thing. In fact, he never even mentioned the incident. He didn't have to, because I'd gotten the message. I never took the car to San Francisco again."

Merv Griffin knew at an early age that he wanted to be in show business, although he was never quite sure exactly *what* he wanted to do in that field. To prepare himself, he did a school play ("It was called *Family Portrait*, and I did two parts—Mordecai and Mendel. I

28

ab-libbed the whole thing. Never learned my lines. The teacher was so angry that she gave me an F.''); sang on the street during the forties to sell War Bonds; presented shows at nearby military bases for G.I.s about to be shipped to the Pacific theater; and played pipe organ at St. Matthew's church, as well as directing the choir.

"I'd make extra money playing organ and singing at weddings and funerals," he says. "Weddings were fifteen dollars and funerals [with a sad voice] commanded twenty. I was so busy in June that it was almost impossible to book me."

There was one booking, however, that Merv missed and this oversight was the cause of a few alarming moments sometime later.

The daughter of a prominent San Mateo family was getting married. Needing an organist-singer for the ceremony, the bride's mother phoned the Griffin household to engage the young man's services. He wasn't at home, so the woman left the message with Rita, who, for some unknown reason, forgot to tell him.

Sadly, the day of the wedding arrived and Merv, oblivious to the fact that his talents were desperately needed at the church, wasn't to be found anywhere. The unfortunate girl, perhaps the only bride in the history of St. Matthew's to do so, marched down the aisle—sans music.

Several years passed. Merv was back in Mills Memorial Hospital, undergoing a tonsillectomy. As the ether mask was placed over his face, the female anesthesiologist said, in a very sweet tone: "Merv, do you remember the time you missed my daughter's wedding, and she had to walk down the aisle without any music?"

Griffin still gets chills recollecting this incident. "Her words were the last I heard before I went under. I know

I panicked . . . tried to pull the mask off, but that's the last thing I remember.

"Later, when I was back in my bed, the doctor came in and asked, 'What happened to you in the operating room? You got so violent that we had to hold you down. The poor anesthesiologist has black-and-blue marks all over her arms.'"

" 'That poor anesthesiologist practically frightened me to death,' I told him."

Merv graduated from San Mateo High in 1942. He was seventeen years old and immediately went to work in the Stores Department at Hunter's Point Naval Station. It was his job to help determine which provisions would be loaded on transport ships headed for the war in the Pacific. During this period he attended San Mateo Junior College for awhile, majoring in music.

While he was working at the Point and going to school, Merv and a girl named Barbara McNutt were heard on a local (KFRC) radio show—"Budda's Amateur Hour" hosted by Dean Maddox. Merv played the piano and the couple sang a medley of patriotic (mostly George M. Cohan) and love songs. Remembers Griffin: "Barbara was just as heavy as I. We must have looked rather bizarre to the studio audience—like Tweedle Dum and Tweedle Dee—standing in front of them singing 'Cuban Love Songs' together."

Nevertheless, they won first prize and were invited back to compete in the finals, judged by professional performers Gertrude Niesen and Billy "Sneezy" Gilbert.

"We lost that one," says Merv. "We placed second. I think first prize went to a one-legged whistler, or *something* like that."

Shortly after this radio exposure, Griffin obtained a job at the San Francisco headquarters of Bank of

30

America. He'd acquired the position with the help of the institution's founder, A.P. Gianni, who lived in San Mateo and was acquainted with Merv and his family.

"I didn't last very long there," he muses. "I worked in the mail room and employees weren't allowed to use the elevator. Can you imagine this two hundred and forty pound butterball running up and down eleven flights of steps all day long?"

Mervyn, Senior, who then taught tennis at the Crocker Estate, got Merv a thirty-dollar-a-week job in the Crocker Bank's checking department. One day Merv was comparing salaries with a fellow employee, who was making sixty dollars per week.

"That's not a lot of money," commented Griffin.

His colleague seemed to take offense at the remark. "What do you mean?" he said. "It's taken me *twelve years* to get my salary to this point."

That's all Merv needed to hear. He went right upstairs and quit.

Another event occurred about this time in Merv's existence. It made him forsake a banking career in favor of an all-out crusade to make a name for himself in the entainment world. The incident took place on his eighteenth birthday. "I was walking down the San Mateo railroad tracks," he recalls, "when, all of a sudden, there was, what seemed like a 'voice' inside me that said: 'From this moment on, your life will never be your own again.' "

Griffin was not really involved in any show business activities at the time, yet he knew that this "very strong thought, which seemed to come out of nowhere," was urging him to enter that profession.

Merv: "I don't believe in revelations or the occult, but that occurrence had a great influence on me and what I decided to do with my life."

He began seeking work as a piano player earning

some money by entertaining at local dances. Then, when he was nineteen, Merv, accompanied by Cal Tjader, was driving past KFRC—the station on which he'd scored in the amateur show—and, on a whim, decided to go in and audition for a staff musician job. (The station, an affiliate of the Mutual Network, boasted such prominent alumni as Art Linkletter, network executive Pat Weaver, and game show producer Mark Goodson.)

There were no openings for piano players, but the station did need a singer for its daily "San Francisco Sketchbook" show. Griffin was about to depart when Tjader, recalling his pal's soprano voice from high school, piped in with, "Merv's a singer."

Merv threw his friend a dirty look, but, since he had nothing to lose, decided to try his hand as a crooner. Fortunately, the passing of a few years had lowered his voice to baritone status. That, and the deft imitation he did of Dick Haymes singing "Sleigh Ride in July," convinced the station management that he was perfect for the job.

He guest starred on "San Francisco Sketchbook" on a Thursday. His salary was one hundred dollars for that show. By the following Monday, his employers were so impressed with his talent that they changed the name of this morning program to "The Merv Griffin Show," backing their new star with a twenty-piece orchestra.

Paul Spiegel of the *Chronicle* liked the fifteen minute daily entertainment and, as a result of a number of columns he wrote praising it, the show, which was heard over forty-four Mutual/Don Lee stations, now was picked up by the entire Mutual network and broadcast transcontinentally, including New York City.

Merv and some friends put together a company called Panda Records, for which Merv cut an album that included numbers like "Sand," "Lullaby of the

Leaves," "Let There Be Love," and "Falling in Love with Love."

The San Mateo boy's income climbed to eleven hundred, then fifteen hundred dollars per week. He started living it up: "I bought two cars and joined three country clubs. My father thought I must be peddling dope on the side."

Mervyn, Senior, who was then working for a stock and bond firm, did, indeed, wonder how his son could be earning more money than he. "It always remained a sore spot with Dad," says Merv.

Weekends, Merv would take the radio orchestra (the regular conductor preferred to relax on his days off) and entertain at various society functions that were scheduled for the Bay Area, thereby adding to his local celebrity status. The drummer for the group was none other than Cal Tjader.

Despite his success, Merv wisely realized his limitations as a singer and studied voice with popular San Francisco coach Bill Stoker, a Mormon who had once sang with the Kay Kyser orchestra. Two of the instructor's other successful students were Johnny Mathis and Guy Mitchell. "After class," Merv recalls, "Guy (who was then known as Al Cernick) and I would sit around and tell each other what we wanted to do."

At KFRC and on the network, Merv Griffin was billed as "America's Romantic Singing Star"—forty-four-inch waist, acne-filled complexion, and all. Naturally, since the reality did not match the image, management took special steps to insure that their listeners' illusions were not shattered. Photos of the artist were not mailed out to fans, nor was there a studio audience at broadcasts. The station heads certainly did everything in their power to make their star's actual looks the best kept secret since the Manhattan Project.

Of course, Griffin wasn't the only radio personality

to have a false image. William Conrad of television's "Cannon" series played "Matt Dillon" when "Gunsmoke" was on the radio, and Gale Gordon, Lucille Ball's favorite boss, was the medium's first "Flash Gordon."

A series of incidents convinced Merv that he had to change his eating habits. The first occurred when movie producer Bill Dozier drove up to San Francisco to meet this new singing sensation who had captured the imagination of housewives all over the country. With that kind of charisma, Griffin could very well be a prime candidate for super-stardom—at least that's what the film-maker thought *before* he met the crooner in person.

When the jarring confrontation did take place, Dozier and his wife, actress Joan Fontaine, had great difficulty in suppressing their laughter. They had, after all, expected "America's Romantic Singing Star" to be more like Clark Gable than Lou Costello.

"I knew what would happen the moment Dozier saw me," claims Merv, "but I went along with the gag, and that's all it amounted to. He couldn't put me in pictures."

A later event was even more humiliating for the rather rotund baritone. "One of my fans, a little old lady who was determined to get a look at me, managed to get into the station through a back entrance. She was standing at the reception desk when I happened to walk by. A secretary said, 'Merv, there's a long distance call for you in your office.'

"The woman looked at me intently, then, in a somewhat disappointed tone of voice, asked: 'Are *you* Merv Griffin?'

"I said, 'Yes,' and she got hysterical. The sight of huge me destroyed her imagination, and she couldn't stop howling."

34

That same week, Joan Edwards, a guest on Merv's show, collared him after he'd signed-off and said, "Look, boy, I think your singing is the end. But that blubber has got to go."

That did it. Griffin decided to diet, consuming only high protein foods. "I ate nothing but steak and salad. Sometimes I'd just have one or the other, and there were even occasions when a meal would only consist of a few lettuce leaves."

It was simply a matter of will power—mind against stomach. The mind won and, within four months, the star had shed eighty pounds. Buying all those new clothes in smaller sizes may have hurt his pocketbook, but Merv looked and felt great.

The year: 1948. Handsome, talented, *slim* Merv Griffin was one of the most popular personalities on San Francisco's entertainment scene, and he had an impressive national radio following also.

Still, he was dissatisfied. He'd climbed as far as he could in this exciting, albeit limited, city. If he was to achieve greater success, it would have to be in the world beyond that which he had already traveled during his twenty-two years. Surprisingly, except for the vacations in Sonora, Yosemite, and Los Angeles, Merv had never been out of the Bay Area.

There was also a personal reason motivating the aspiring Mr. Griffin to leave his home base. Since high school, he'd been going steady with an attractive young lady named Gypsy Ernst. The romance had grown to the point where, if it continued much longer, marriage would be the only logical result. He cared for the girl, but Merv wasn't about to make a permanent commitment then. His father had married young and, despite the fact it was a happy union, he had cut his promising career as a professional tournament tennis player short. Merv didn't want the same fate to befall his designs on show business; therefore flight seemed the most logical solution.

So, when the all-important chance for advancement presented itself the year Truman defeated Dewey, Merv was ready for it. Whereas this move was to result in the ripening of his talent and the acquisition of worldly knowledge, it also set him smack in the middle of a once-prospering area of entertainment which was rapidly on its way to becoming an anachronism.

Two

It was an age of excitement and it lasted more than three decades, seeing us through the Roaring Twenties, the Great Depression, and the Second World War. Terms like "symphonic jazz," "syncopation," "improvisation," and "swing" became part of our everyday vocabulary while men like Whiteman, Pollack, Goodman, the Dorseys, and Miller were making their bids for immortality. It was a period that saw what was perhaps the most dramatic and influential changes in the annuals of popular music. This was the era of the great dance bands.

Historians have never really agreed as to which leader had the first *organized* dance group. However, garnering a significant number of votes for this honor is Art Hickman, who assembled his first band in 1913—about the time the foxtrot was becoming fashionable.

Art was a baseball fan, hanging around the training camp of the San Francisco Seals. This particular season he approached Dell Howard, the team manager, with the idea of getting together a group of musicians, with himself as leader, to entertain the team during the evenings. Howard liked the suggestion and gave Art the go-ahead.

Hickman's band was quite popular at the camp and, because of the considerable publicity given it by the newspapermen who were covering the team's activities, soon found itself booked into San Francisco's posh St. Francis Hotel. The group's reputation grew, as did its size. Indeed, with a roster of ten, it was possibly the largest group of its day.

Florenz Ziegfeld heard them play in 1919 and signed the band to come to New York for a featured spot in the 1920 edition of his *Follies*. The following year, Hickman's group—unique in its use of string bass, instead of the more usual tuba or bass brass—opened the Coconut Grove at the Ambassador Hotel in Los Angeles.

Though he was always a huge success in his engagements, Art became bored with the dance band business and retired shortly after the Los Angeles date, turning his orchestra over to Frank Ellis. He died in 1930.

There were other groups of note that began during those early years. Ted Lewis, a successful vaudeville performer, formed his own orchestra in 1916, as did King Oliver, Paul Specht, and Fred Waring, whose initial undertaking was a six-man string group, which he tagged "Waring's Banjatrazz." However, it wasn't until the early twenties that the dance band became a truly viable force on the American entertainment scene.

Until that time, the only methods by which a particular group could be exposed to the public was through personal appearances or recordings. The record business was thriving then, although its product was quite crude by today's standards.

Radio was the factor that radically altered the times. Early in the 1920s, technological developments in this relatively new method of mass communication enabled manufacturers of radio sets to market them at a price that a majority of the population could afford. Sixty million dollars was spent on radio sets during 1922 alone and, by 1930, that annual figure had climbed to over eight hundred million.

With the wireless becoming an integral part of

American life, it wasn't long before major networks were created with facilities for transmitting programs coast-to-coast. This development allowed bands that were being heard regularly on local or regional stations to gain national reputations almost overnight. Most of the leading orchestras of the twenties had their own sponsored programs, drawing large listening audiences who were anxious to hear their favorite groups in person.

Another meaningful trend that began around this period was the movement of dancing out of the various lodges and community halls and into ballrooms built particularly for that purpose. Leading hotels also found it profitable to provide dancing facilities for their patrons. As ballrooms grew in number, so did the orchestras—traveling around the country in cramped buses—to play in these halls.

New York, with its top hotels and Broadway shows—which occasionally utilized the services of bands—became the hub of this frenzied activity. Most of the recordings also came out of the Big Apple, although this industry suffered tremendously from the advent of radio until new technical advances improved the product a few years later.

Many bandleaders who prospered during this decade of bootleg gin and the corner speakeasy have etched a place for themselves in the history books. Names like Red Nichols, Ben Bernie, Kay Kyser, Isham Jones, Carleton Coon and Joe Sanders' Nighthawks, Jan Garber, Rudy Vallee, Fletcher Henderson, Guy Lombardo, Ted Weems, and Louis "Sachmo" Armstrong are synonymous with the period. Yet, there are two whose stars rose above the rest—Paul Whiteman and Ben Pollack.

Whiteman, dubbed the "King of Jazz," hailed from Denver, Colorado, and was the son of a director of musical education for that city's public schools. Moving to San Francisco in 1911, he worked with various groups until, while visiting a dive on the Barbary Coast, he first heard what was called "jazz." To him, a trained musician, it sounded crude and unusual, but was, at the same time, rhythmic and fascinating. Paul decided to capture the improvised strains he'd heard and place them within an orchestrated framework, thereby creating what was to become known as "symphonic jazz." Unfortunately, it would be a few years before his dream was fully realized.

After a stint as musical director for the U.S. Navy, where he headed a forty-piece band, and civilian engagements in some of the country's leading hotels, Whiteman entered the recording field with his popular, albeit conventional, group, and soon had made a version of "Whispering" which sold an unheard of 1.8 million copies.

Bookings at New York's Palais Royal—to play for audiances like the Vanderbilts—and the Palace Theater followed, as did an appearance in *George White's Scandals of 1922*. Then came London and the Hippodrome. By the time he returned home, Whiteman was, without doubt, the hottest thing in the business.

Nevertheless, the overweight musician was not satisfied. He still had visions of making his "symphonic jazz" a reality, conceiving the then revolutionary plan of leading a large orchestra in a jazz concert at a symphony hall.

The historic occasion took place in New York City at Aeolian Hall on February 12, 1924. Fronting a twenty-three-piece orchestra, Whiteman offered George Gershwin's audiences a combination of standard tunes like "Whispering"; a few pieces containing a contrast of "legitimate" and "jazz" scoring; some semi-symphonic arrangements; and, at the piano, performed his new composition, "Rhapsody in Blue." The concert was an overwhelming success and was later repeated at both Carnegie Hall and London's Albert Hall, where the program was changed somewhat. From that point, Whiteman's group became less of a dance band and more of a show band, playing both semi-classic and popular selections in future engagements.

Although Whiteman's title as the "King of Jazz" was probably a misnomer in that he seldom allowed his musicians to depart from their set arrangements (certain soloists, like legendary cornetist Bix Beiderbecke and the Dorsey brothers, were later exceptions), his demand for a high quality of performance and his use of only top instrumentalists certainly helped to raise the level of popular music during his day, and gained him a strong following which has sustained itself through the years.

As opposed to Whiteman's practices, Ben Pollack's band was one of the first groups in the United States that allowed its jazz soloists a high degree of freedom. Pollack, a talented drummer, was born in Chicago, but it was in California during 1925 that he formed his own band. That summer, he acquired the services of a teenaged clarinetist named Benny Goodman. The group traveled for the next couple of years, working various clubs around the country. Finally, they wound up in New York, found a place at the Park Central Hotel and, later, the Silver Slipper nightclub. Pollack's roster of musicians at that time included Jimmy McPartland, Gil Rodin, and Glenn Miller, who, apart from playing the trombone, did occasional arrangements for the band. Indeed, Pollack was responsible for "discovering" many instrumentalists—in addition to Miller and Goodman—who subsequently became more famous than he. These finds included Jack Teagarden and Harry James.

But Ben was more interested in becoming a show

business personality than in making good music—a desire that conflicted with the aims of those who worked under him—and he found it difficult to maintain a stable personnel within his orchestra for any long period of time. Musicians would depart his ranks to either join other groups or form their own.

Pollack eventually gave up the drums, and ended his career as a front man for different orchestras. Though his personal contributions to the advancement of popular music were slight, his ability to uncover, nurture and exploit new talent was exceptional, introducing to the world some of the greatest pop artists of that, or any, generation.

In 1929 Wall Street laid its mammoth egg and the entertainment industry, along with the public at large, fought to survive the Depression that followed. Record companies went bankrupt. Bands folded. Yet a good many of the more popular groups remained, catering to people's needs for escapism during this bleak period.

Another significant occurrence—the repeal of Prohibition in 1933—had a strong, positive effect on the music business, in that it allowed speakeasies to convert into respectable nightclubs, and gave hotels extra much-needed revenue with which they could hire the leading orchestras to entertain their customers. Record companies were also helped at this time by the development of the jukebox and its subsequent integration into virtually every community in America. Disc sales increased; the way was paved for the creation of the "Hit Parade."

Prior to the summer of 1935, the bands that had become well-established during the twenties assumed a safe, conservative profile, concentrating on rather conventional dance material, instead of branching out in any new musical directions. Although orchestras like those led by Glen Gray, the Dorsey brothers, and

Lawrence Welk were admirable in their high degree of technical skill, the music they played made little demands on the attention of its listeners.

The event that changed everything took place on the evening of August 21, 1935 at the Palomar Ballroom in Los Angeles. Benny Goodman, who, after leaving Pollack, had worked for leaders like Whiteman, Ted Lewis, and Red Nichols, was fronting his own orchestra, and this engagement was coming at the conclusion of a disastrous cross-country tour. The respected clarinetist had decided to form this group because he wanted to play music that had more life to it, rather than the same standard arrangements being offered by his contemporaries. However, dance hall owners wanted a band that played "sweet" music—like that of Guy Lombardo—and they invariably complained to Goodman that he was playing too loud.

By the time the group reached Los Angeles, Goodman knew he was in financial trouble and that it was unlikely he'd be able to hold his men together beyond this date. He decided to go for broke and, utilizing the innovative arrangements he'd purchased from Fletcher Henderson, cut loose one evening—despite protests from the management.

The patrons stopped dancing and just listened. They'd never heard a wild sound like this before and were enthralled by it. "Swing" was being born that night and, before long, it would sweep the country, completely revolutionizing the world of popular music.

At the end of the thirties, the band business was again a healthy one. Record sales were good, groups could be heard all over the radio dial, and in-person engagements were plentiful. A host of top talent—most of whom leaned toward the freedom of "swing"—had risen from the wings, with names like Artie Shaw, Bob Crosby, Woody Herman, Charlie Barnett, Sammy Kaye, and two former Goodman sidemen, Gene Krupa and Harry James, joining the ranks of the more popular leaders of the day.

Band vocalists began to achieve individual followings about this time and, in many instances, had a box-office appeal equal to the orchestras with whom they were featured. Most successful of the singers was, of course, Frank Sinatra, who was with Tommy Dorsey's group.

The coming of the Second World War put an end to the spectacular expansion that the band and record businesses had been enjoying. Record production was cut some seventy percent because the shellac needed for their manufacture came from India and the government needed the bulk of what was able to be imported through enemy lines for war production. The draft took its toll on musicians also. Not holding essential occupations, sidemen were fair game for induction and, during the peak war period, many orchestras had problems finding suitable replacements for their missing members.

While this was going on, the type of music being played was changing. Although "swing" was still with us, most of the big bands added several sentimental ballads to their repertoire.

Dominating the music scene, along with Goodman and Lombardo, during the forties were the Dorsey brothers and Glenn Miller.

Jimmy and Tommy Dorsey—admired by their contemporaries for their mastery of the alto saxophone and trombone, respectively—had formed their own group in 1934. Unfortunately, the music they played together was a mishmash—a jumble of Dixieland scores, straight ballads, and an occasional preview of the adventurous "swing." This lack of direction was attributable to the temperamental differences of the brothers, which resulted in Tommy's exiting the group one night in 1935 during a performance.

Jimmy retained most of the group's musicians and his band was quite successful, adopting a style that included two-beat instrumentals and commercial ballads. His 1941 recording of "Green Eyes," featuring vocals by Bob Eberly and Helen O'Connell, has become a classic.

After departing his brother's company, Tommy Dorsey formed his own orchestra and chose to follow a swing-oriented policy. Considered by many critics to have been more of a perfectionist than his brother, the band leader wisely capitalized on the services of Frank Sinatra for the three years the singer was under contract to him, recording such hits as "I'll Never Smile Again," "Hear My Song," and "Violetta."

The Fabulous Dorseys did not stay apart professionally forever, but joined forces again in 1953, recording together for three years.

Like Tommy Dorsey, Glenn Miller had a reputation for being a musical perfectionist. He'd been a sought-after arranger and trombonist since the twenties, and worked for such leaders as Abe Lyman, Ben Pollack, the Dorsey brothers, and Red Nichols. Nevertheless, it was not until 1937 that he formed his own orchestra, employing the unique new sound (reed voicing, with clarinet over four saxes) he'd taken years to develop in his mind and which would become his trademark.

Success did not come quickly for Miller. His first group was disbanded after a year, but, by mid-1938, he'd started up again, hiring, as he'd done previously, the best instrumentalists available. This time, however, the initial public response was no better than with the first venture.

The big break came in 1939 when the orchestra played the Glenn Island Casino in New Rochelle, a gig that included ten weekly radio broadcasts, giving them their widest exposure to date. Overnight, Glenn Miller became the most sought-after attraction in popular music, breaking attendance records wherever he appeared and cutting discs that hit the top of the charts.

Volunteering for the armed forces in 1942, Major Glenn Miller organized the AAF Orchestra, which played for servicemen throughout the United States and Britain. In December of 1944, he took off with three others for Paris, planning to make final arrangements for his group to tour service camps. The plane disappeared over the English Channel without a trace.

Glenn Miller was dead, but the legend remained. No musical style of the band era retained its appeal for as long as that created by Miller. Tunes like "Moonlight Serenade," "Little Brown Jug," "Tuxedo Junction," "In the Mood," and many others are still played today by bands that specialize in recreating the Miller sound.

Despite manpower shortages and gasoline rationing, which made it difficult for groups to travel, the war years were a boom period for the band business. Indeed, with the populace spending as if there were no tomorrow, the entire entertainment industry prospered.

But the good times didn't last.

Once the conflicts in Europe and the Pacific ended and the musicians in uniform began to return home, established leaders who'd been away quickly reformed their orchestras and attempted to regain any ground they'd lost during the war years. There were also new names, like Ray Anthony and Buddy Rich, coming up in the field, each striving for their share of the post-war entertainment dollar.

Sadly, that dollar was in a steadily diminishing flow. With the boys home from the war, people didn't spend money as recklessly as they had when futures were uncertain. Now there were families to start and homes and furniture to buy. Paychecks had to go for the *necessities* of life.

By the middle of 1946, attendance had started an irreversible decline in both ballrooms and nightclubs. Engagements became fewer and, before long, many bands were folding. In an attempt to hold off the inevitable, several of the top-name orchestras cut down their personnel, agreed to accept smaller guarantees from the dance promoters, and insisted that ballroom admission prices be scaled down so that they were within the reach of the average wage-earners.

In 1948—while the orchestra leaders were waging their valiant, if futile, battle to save this once lucrative business—Merv Griffin made his entry into the dance field as a vocalist and sideman. He couldn't have arrived at a worse time.

The man responsible for bringing Merv into this terminally ill industry was Freddy Martin, a society band leader with a winning personality. Although popular for his very listenable style, he had never quite reached the musical heights occupied by giants like Goodman and Miller.

Born in Cleveland in 1908, Martin was raised in an orphanage after the death of both parents. He studied the C-melody saxophone, then played with local orchestras, where he became friendly with Guy Lombardo, who encouraged him to form his own group.

Freddy's initial success as the leader of a six-piece band was in 1931 at Brooklyn's Bossert Hotel and resulted in his securing a recording contract with the Brunswick label. Later, he affiliated with RCA Victor.

Martin hit his stride in 1941 when he seized on the idea of adopting classical melodies to popular dance tempos. Perhaps his best-known effort in this area is his version of Tchaikovsky's "B Flat Minor Piano Concerto," which he retitled "Tonight We Love."

While his orchestra was playing one of its many

return engagements at the St. Francis Hotel in San Francisco, Martin was faced with the problem of finding a new male singer. Stuart Wade, who'd held that position, had decided to try his hand at an acting career and given notice.

The call for a replacement went out. Freddy began listening to demo records (supplied by song publishers to promote new tunes in their respective catalogues), searching for a singer with vocal qualities that would complement his group's musical style. Ultimately, the choice was narrowed down to two possibilities and Martin asked Jean Barry, his secretary, to hear the records and make the final choice.

Miss Barry's selection was Merv Griffin, whom she'd often listened to on the radio when she was in San Francisco. Coincidentally, Martin would also tune in that KFRC morning show during his stays on the west coast.

On Freddy's instructions, the secretary contacted Griffin and set up a lunch date. As she recalls the meeting: "Merv was a very personable fellow and I liked him immediately. But, since he hadn't traveled outside of San Francisco or Los Angeles, he was also quite green and naive."

Merv sang "Where or When" at his audition and Martin was impressed, although he did think the vocalist needed to lose some weight. "You should have seen me before," said Merv, who assured Freddy he would maintain a strict diet.

The orchestra leader offered Griffin a five-year contract with his group as vocalist and second piano player—the first such bid he'd ever made to an artist. Merv's salary was to be $175 per week, with twenty-five-dollar raises every thirteen weeks.

"At first I laughed at the suggestion," recalls Merv, "because the money was less than the fifteen hundred per week I was then making. However, I quickly reconsidered when I learned that we'd be playing New York and other big cities throughout the country."

Griffin began his tenure with Martin while the leader was still appearing at the St. Francis, and continued to do his own nationally broadcast radio show until the orchestra went on tour.

"Merv was very stiff and unanimated when he started with us," says Jean Barry (now the wife of accountant Harold Plant). "He'd had very little experience singing in front of a live audience and wasn't sure how to relate to them.

"To help him overcome the problem, I would go out and stand in the audience, so he'd sing directly to me. Gradually, he began to relax, then his warm personality, which had always been there, came out."

Freddy remembers that Merv used to alter his singing style almost nightly during his first few weeks with the band. "He wasn't sure what his style should be, so he'd listen to records every afternoon, then come in and sing like the last vocalist he'd heard. One night, he'd sound like Crosby, and the next he'd be Perry Como. We kidded him a lot about this, but he was just trying to find the sound that worked best for him."

The leader also discovered that his singer had a very awkward waddling walk, a hangover from the fat days, and looked rather silly when he came on stage: "I decided to have him make his entrance during a blackout. The announcer would say, 'Ladies and gentlemen . . . Merv Griffin.' Then, the lights would come on and, if he hadn't stumbled while getting there, Merv was at the microphone, ready to sing."

When Martin's orchestra left San Francisco to begin a nationwide tour, Griffin quit his radio job and bid goodbye to his family, as well as Miss Gypsy Ernst. However, just before the group departed, Rita Griffin and her two sisters summoned Jean Barry, who, by this time, had become a close friend of the vocalist. ("There was never any romance between Merv and me," she explains. "We were just good pals and always laughed at the same things.")

Merv's family gave Jean some money and made her promise that, on his birthday, she would get him a cake and throw a little party. "What they really were saying," laughs Jean, "was, 'Please take care of our baby.' "

The day he hit twenty-three, Merv was in Prairie du Chien, Wisconsin, doing a one-night gig. "The band bus arrived in this little town at about four in the afternoon," recalls Jean. "After checking in at the hotel, I made a mad dash to find a bakery. I set up the surprise party for Merv in the hotel dining room and the guys in the band, many of whom were amused by the corniness of the whole thing, helped me pull it off. Merv was overjoyed."

The tour, from its start, proved to be a grueling one for all involved, especially for Merv, who'd never lived on a bus before. Leaving San Francisco, the group played a series of one-night stands that ran for seventy-four consecutive nights. The first night off was in the "lively" community of Fargo, North Dakota, where Griffin spent the evening viewing Clifton Webb in *Sitting Pretty* at the local movie house.

To avoid going bananas while riding from town to town on that stuffy, crowded bus, Merv would constantly enlist his fellow sidemen in a series of word games such as Hangman or Twenty Questions. He'd always enjoyed contests of the mind and, perhaps, these on-the-road time-killers helped condition his imagination for the television game shows he would develop later in his career.

Jean and Merv both found humor in the most foolish

things, so it wasn't unusual to see the pair laughing uproariously on the bus. She remembers: "When you're moving eight hours a day, day after day, it's very easy to get silly. Merv and I were big laughers and, more than once, we wound up on the floor, holding our sides.

"Freddy was always annoyed with us. He's an avid reader and we kept disturbing him."

Johnny Cochran, a trombone player for Martin, remembers that Merv had "a fantastic facility for repeating everything someone said. He used to tease Jean Barry by immediately repeating her like a tape recorder. Everybody on the bus found his routine very funny, because they sounded just like two magpies."

Few who rode the Martin bus in the course of the four years Merv was on the team will forget a particular sideman who was always drunk and was also very shy. "He was so bashful," claims Griffin, "that he never even spoke up when he had to go to the bathroom."

In order to relieve his immediate problem, the poor musician would borrow a hat from the overhead rack, utilize it as a urinal, then replace it. Everything would be cool until the bus hit a bump and the receptacle tipped over. Freddy was furious the day the liquid trickled into his briefcase and ruined his business papers.

Martin, himself, was the catalyst of one rather humiliating episode.

The orchestra had been playing a date in Windsor, Ontario, and was on its way back to the United States. Stopped at Canadian Customs, a government agent was asking the group some routine questions. When it came Griffin's turn to answer, the singer informed the officer that he had not made any purchases in Canada. At that point, Martin, who'd had a drink or two, shouted, "Show him the diamonds, Merv!"

The Federal man found no amusement in Freddy's crack and the bus stayed at the border for four hours while it was searched thoroughly.

Ninety one-nighters after leaving San Francisco, Martin and company arrived in New York City—Gotham—the Big Apple. Like any other normal human being seeing this fantastic city for the first time—especially at sunrise from the New Jersey side—Merv was overwhelmed. He couldn't believe that anything could be that beautiful. "I was a total hick," he readily admits when describing how he tried to see all the sights his first day there.

Following an engagement at the Waldorf-Astoria, the band was booked into the Strand Theater to entertain between screenings of *Johnny Belinda*, the Academy Award-winning feature starring Jane Wyman in the role of a deaf mute.

The first performance of this three-week engagement played to a packed, albeit *unusual*, house. Merv came out to open the show with one of his best numbers ("Because") and, after he was finished, received a very distressing response from the audience. In fact, there was no response at all.

Peering into the darkened auditorium, Griffin soon discovered *why* he'd drawn such a cold reaction. The entire audience was talking—in *sign language*. As a publicity gimmick, the theater management had invited members of an organization for the deaf to the Wyman picture and had neglected to inform Martin. The spectators could read the lips of the movie actors, but they could not hear the live music and singing.

The *New York Daily Mirror*, in a review of the Strand show, wrote: "Merv Griffin is a brilliant baritone. He croons 'Because,' the rhythmic 'Pecos Bill' novelty, and 'Miserlou' to show off a good voice in the different tempos, plus strong personality."

Between performances, Merv would often catch a breath of fresh air in the alley behind the Strand. There, night after night, he chatted with a young actor who always parked his motorcycle in the alley that also serviced the Ethel Barrymore Theater. This pensive performer was appearing in the hit play at the Barrymore—Tennessee Williams' *A Streetcar Named Desire*. His name was Marlon Brando.

"I really liked Marlon," says Merv, "and, first chance I got, bought a ticket to see his show.

"I was stunned by it, particularly since I really thought I was going to see a musical. I'd been so out of it all my life in San Mateo, that watching a powerhouse play like this really shocked me.

"While I was in New York, I also went to see *Guys and Dolls*. Again, I was bewildered. I was completely unfamiliar with Damon Runyon lingo and didn't understand a word the actors were saying.

"I was a real 'farmer.' "

Early in November of 1948, the Martin troupe was back on the bus, doing their inevitable series of one-nighters, on their way to a four-month engagement at the fabulous Coconut Grove in Los Angeles.

This legendary night spot, located in the Ambassador Hotel, was a prime gathering place for the elite of Hollywood society. Virtually every evening, top film stars, producers, and directors were at front row tables dining, drinking, and enjoying only the best acts in the nightclub field. Among the most popular attractions to often play the Grove was Freddy Martin and his Orchestra. Indeed, years later, the leader and his group would become the nitery's "house" orchestra.

Merv, to say the least, was in awe of celebrities. He was also ambitious. So, between sets, the singer would usually go out into the house to mix with the rich and the famous. Johnny Cochran: "He was—and still is—a charming guy, who could talk his way into any situation. Every night he'd get off the bandstand, walk up to a table of strangers (naturally, it was the most 'important' table in the room), and, a minute later, be invited to sit down. Merv made a lot of good contacts this way. The VIPs liked him immediately."

One of Griffin's most avid fans back in those nostalgic days was none other than the very elusive Howard Hughes. The eccentric billionaire would sit in the back of the Grove, eating vanilla ice cream, while Merv sang.

During his initial period with Martin, Merv dated a girl named Jay Hall, but this relationship evaporated after he was introduced to a bright and lovely young redhead named Judy Balaban, the daughter of powerful New York-based Paramount Pictures executive, Barney Balaban.

The couple met at a party while the orchestra was making one of its frequent visits to the Big Town. They tcok to each other immediately, but, regrettably, the next day, Merv had to leave Manhattan to continue his tour.

Shortly thereafter, the band was playing a date near the University of Florida when, who should appear on the scene but Miss Balaban. She was in town visiting her brother, a student at that college, and, hearing that Martin was there, decided to stop by to say "Hello."

Merv and Judy began seeing each other on a steady basis. They had fun together—"wonderful, wild times." In fact, when the orchestra started on the road again, Judy, who loved the show business life, tagged along to keep her new beau company.

A favorite pastime of the couple was to pool their crazy senses of humor in devising some of the wackiest gags their friends had ever seen. At one formal party, for example, the pair arrived at the door looking very elegant—*except* for the oversized rubber feet they were wearing.

Another stunt Merv and Judy came up with became the inspiration for a Red Skelton routine. The couple was throwing a party for the band at the Balaban family apartment, where Judy lived. Knowing that Freddy would probably be late because he'd stopped off to have a drink or two, the host and hostess, with the help of the other guests, turned all the furniture in the living room on its side, then sat in the chairs, pretending nothing was amiss. According to one guest: "Freddy came in, saw the whole topsy-turvy world, and, right there and then, swore he'd never touch another drink."

Merv and Judy were an accepted couple in the show business crowd and most of their friends expected that they would marry sooner or later. However, the Balabans were Jewish. Merv was not. As far as Barney Balaban was concerned, no gentile—especially an Irish Catholic—was going to marry his daughter.

But the parents realized that they couldn't push Judy. If they did, she might up and marry "that *goy* band singer" out of spite. No, for the time being, at least, they'd be nice to Merv and let the relationship play itself out. Hopefully, the girl would get over her "infatuation."

In the meantime, Griffin was "paying his dues" as an entertainer, making good contacts for future use, and formulating in his mind the next step he would take in his career. He wouldn't be ready to leave Martin for quite awhile as there was still much to be gained through this association. But he realized that with the band business having fallen upon hard times, he would, ultimately, have to make a move forward, lest he go down with what he knew was a sinking ship.

February 1949 had found the Martin orchestra again in San Francisco at the St. Francis. While he was back on his old stomping grounds, Merv, accompanied by pianist and orchestra leader Jack Fina, returned to his alma mater, San Mateo High, to put on a special show for the sophomore and freshman classes.

Martin, with Griffin as his lead soloist, was at the St. Francis again in late November of 1950. This time, some two hundred citizens of San Mateo, headed by Mayor Carrol M. Spears, honored the two entertainers at a special party in the hotel's Mural Room. Both were given honorary memberships in the chamber of commerce, as well as gold keys to the city.

A month later, Merv entered Mills Memorial Hospital in San Mateo to have his tonsils removed.

While Merv was appearing at the St. Francis, he became the "willing" victim of a nightly practical joke, courtesy of his good friend, Jean Barry, some members of the band, and the hotel waiters.

One of the vocalist's numbers was a hit novelty song, entitled "The Thing," which told of a man who discovered a mysterious box on the beach and found that its contents (never revealed in the lyrics) made him an outcast of society. Griffin utilized a prop box for his rendition of the tune, and, at the end of the piece, would open it and look inside.

What Merv did find inside each night was bizarre enough to "destroy" the demeanor of any entertainer. "Raw eels, piles of messy garbage, Tampax covered with tomato paste, and dog crap," according to a chuckling Griffin, "were just some of the foul, disgusting things that Jean and the waiters put into that box. Even though I was expecting *something* to be awaiting me when I opened it, it was impossible to keep a straight face once the moment actually came."

Griffin had a recording date in Los Angeles and chose to drive down in his own car, rather than ride the band bus. On impulse, he decided to look up his old high school friend, Bob Murphy, who was then a sophomore in pre-law at the University of San Francisco.

"I was in the middle of a mid-term exam," recalls Murph, "when Merv drove his car up in front of the portable classroom and began honking the horn. I couldn't imagine what he wanted, so I excused myself from the test and went out to see.

" 'I'm going down to L.A. to record with Freddy,' he said. 'Come on along. We'll have fun.'

"It was a nutty thing for me to do, but I got into the car and off we went. On the drive down, Merv said, 'You know, someday I'm going to be a big star and, when I am, I want you to work for me. You'll be my attorney.' "

As Murphy would find out years later, Merv Griffin was not one to make idle promises.

The four years he spent with Freddy Martin gave Merv the opportunity to cut many records with the orchestra, three of which went on to become major hits. "Wilhelmina," and "Never Been Kissed" sold about a half million copies each, but a novelty number by Englishman Fred Hetherton, which Griffin sang with a cockney accent, hit the three million mark. The title: "I've Got a Lovely Bunch of Coconuts."

Sadly, Merv did not share in that financial bonanza. Since he was under contract to the orchestra leader, he was paid a flat fee of fifty dollars for his contribution. Nevertheless, the success of this 1951 disc served to motivate RCA Victor to give the promising young singer his own solo recording contract.

Years later, Merv would say of "Coconuts": "That thing embarrassed me. What talent did that take? It was all gimmicked up. Phony. Fake."

In 1950, Griffin made his motion picture debut in a fifteen-minute short for Universal-International—*Music by Martin*. Freddy and his orchestra were, of course, the stars of this well done entertainment, which took only a day to film. Merv's number in the picture was "Tenement Symphony."

The Martin orchestra was featured on a number of local and regional television shows in the early fifties, first originating from San Francisco, then from Los Angeles (broadcast from KTLA). Finally, for twenty-six weeks, they did a national NBC program from New York City. Called "The Hazel Bishop Show," after the name of the sponsor, the thirty-minute program aired live on Wednesday nights at ten and was kinescoped for broadcast on the West Coast two weeks later.

Lyricist Irving Taylor, who, at that time, supplied special material for the Martin group (and who would later supply the words for such song hits as "Everybody Loves Somebody" and "Kookie, Kookie, Lend Me Your Comb") was the producer and head writer for the "Bishop Show," which featured Merv as its lead male singer. Essentially, the program he staged was a pleasant musical interlude, not too dissimilar from the format Lawrence Welk currently employs on his program.

Throughout these infant days of television when everything was done live, embarrassing errors or "bloopers" were an every day occurrence. Credit Merv Griffin with one of the classic goofs in television history. As Taylor recalls the incident:

"Part of Merv's weekly chores was to do the commercial for the new Hazel Bishop non-smear lipstick. The girl doing the spot was to kiss him, then he would wipe his handkerchief across his lips and hold it up for the camera.

"This particular night, he accidentally rubbed some brown make-up off his face, but didn't notice it until it was too late."

Griffin picks up the story: "I looked at the handkerchief as the camera moved in and realized what I'd done. I almost died. As I held it up and said 'Look, no lipstick smear,' I flipped it around real fast with a pleading look on my face and stuffed it back into my pocket. The fact that everybody in the studio was in hysterics certainly didn't help matters.''

The executive from the Bishop company who acted as liaison between the sponsor and the television production staff was a humorless man, who, in this account, will be known as ''Mr. Jones.'' ''He had everybody on the program scared to death,'' says Taylor, ''because he enjoyed firing people at a moment's notice. Even Freddy Martin didn't want to get in his way, since the guy had the power to cancel the series or even replace the star.

''I think the only ones who weren't intimidated by him were Merv and myself—and we were always putting him on.''

Evidently, when the aforementioned non-smear lipstick first came on the market, there were some problems with it. True, it did what it claimed to do (it didn't rub off), but it also caused the lips of many of its users to swell up. People involved with the television show who'd been given free samples of the product began to receive reports from their wives, mothers, and girl friends that the cosmetic was causing them to have an allergic reaction.

At the same time this furor was in progress, Griffin and Taylor happened to bump into Mr. Jones outside the studio. The executive began bragging to them that a national magazine was going to do a study about the revolutionary new lipstick, and that he would like to tie the product in with a big national charity for more publicity.

''Which one?'' asked Merv, a twinkle in his eye. ''Doctor's Hospital?''

The Hazel Bishop company, of course, made some quick changes in the chemical mixture of their product, thus alleviating the problem.

Each week, Martin's program was built around a different theme with musical numbers selected to coincide with that particular motif. The prosaic Mr. Jones, not having learned his lesson from the magazine episode, made the mistake one evening of inquiring of mischievous Griffin and Taylor as to what the next week's theme would be.

"We're doing the show in a whore house," quipped Taylor.

"That's right," agreed Merv, jumping right in. "I'm going to sing tunes like 'All of Me,' 'Body and Soul,' . . . ."

Taylor: "The man looked right at us with no reaction whatsoever. In fact, he was so square that, on one occasion, he came to me and said, 'How come you only do unknown songs on the program?'

"The tunes he was talking about were 'Tea for Two' and 'Stardust,' and the pathetic thing about it was that he was dead serious."

Merv resided at New York's Royalton Hotel while he was doing both the "Bishop Show" and appearing with Martin at the Roosevelt Hotel. He shared these rooms with Robert Clary, the short, French-born actor-entertainer, who shot to fame in Leonard Stillman's *New Faces of 1952*, and, more recently, co-starred in the long-running television series, "Hogan's Heroes."

Griffin had met Clary in 1950 in California, shortly after the Frenchman arrived in this country. Recently signed by Capital Records, Bob, accompanied by publicist Red Doff, went to the Hollywood Palladium to see Freddy Martin. Clary: "After the performance, Merv, who'd heard I was in the audience, came over and introduced himself. He'd heard a recording called 'Put Your Shoes On, Lucy' that I'd made in France—a big hit in the States—and was a fan.

"We hit it right off. The next day, in fact, he introduced me to Natalie Cantor [Eddie's daughter], who was later to become my wife."

Merv saw a lot of Clary while he was on the West Coast and, on one occasion when both were in San Francisco, he invited Bob to his parents' home for dinner. Remembers Griffin: "Bob had never eaten corn-on-the-cob before, so when my mother asked him if he'd like a second piece, he said 'Yes,' and handed her the empty cob for a refill."

The pair spent much time together in New York also, engaging in heavy rap sessions in which each would relate his dreams of major stardom to the other. Watching them walk down the street was, indeed, an amusing sight, since Merv would often make it a point to rest his arm on the pint-sized Clary's head.

Another friendship that Merv developed during those days in New York was with Harry Belafonte, then an unknown jazz vocalist, who, after listening to recordings of African and Caribbean music, had decided to switch his style to that of a folk singer.

The entertainer asked Merv, as a favor, to accompany him to Philadelphia where he was going to break in his new act at a local club. Griffin was to criticize the performance and also offer moral support.

"It was a terrible experience," recalls Merv. "He was great singing songs like 'Matilda,' but all the drunks wanted to hear was 'Melancholy Baby.' Harry was destroyed."

A few weeks later, Merv brought Dave Kapp, an RCA Victor executive, to the Village Vanguard in New York to see Belafonte do his act. Kapp, who now heads his own company, was so impressed that the next day he signed the folk singer to a Victor recording contract.

Harry Belafonte wasn't the last unknown performer whom Merv Griffin would help to achieve success.

By May of 1952, Merv's career was moving forward at a steady clip. Not only was he appearing with Martin at the Rooesvelt Hotel and on television, he also had his own RCA Victor recording contract and was getting various offers to do club and hotel dates as a single, rather than with the celebrated orchestra leader. Then, the inevitable happened. Just when things were going great, he received his draft notice.

With the Korean War in progress, Martin and Griffin realized that there was little chance of the singer getting a deferment. So when their Roosevelt engagement was over, Merv bid good-bye to his employer of four years, who then departed New York to fulfill other commitments. Merv had had his draft records transferred from San Mateo to New York and it was there that he stayed to await his induction date.

June arrived before Merv was called in to take his pre-induction physical and, when the results of the examination were in, he received a pleasant surprise.

He'd flunked!

Due to a mild allergy, and the fact that he was then twenty-six years old (one year over the age being inducted), the army had seen fit to reject him.

The two years of military service were no longer a threat to his career and, therefore, Merv had a decision to make. He could return to his secure place in the Martin troupe, or else venture forth on his own.

Wisely, Merv chose the latter course. Aside from being tired of the eternal bus ride, he knew that the momentum he had gained over the past few years with the orchestra was such that he had a good shot at making it as a single. Martin was a nice man and the relationship had been invaluable to Merv, but to stay with Freddy meant career stagnation, and no performer—ambitious or not—can afford that.

Martin, then appearing in Las Vegas, was both hurt

and angry when he learned of Griffin's decision. "I had big plans for Merv," says Freddy. "After four years, he was the highest paid member of my company. I wanted him to finish his apprenticeship with me—as Sinatra had done with Dorsey—then act as his personal manager.

"He was a fine performer, a wonderful guy, and the public loved him. I really can't blame him for wanting to do better for himself—using the orchestra as a stepping stone. I was unhappy then, but today we're best of friends."

Freddy's initial reaction when he got the bad news had been to consult with his attorney to see if he could hold Griffin to the final year of his five-year contract. The lawyer advised him to drop the matter, however.

The breach between Martin and Griffin did not last for long. While Freddy was still in Vegas (at the Last Frontier), his new male vocalist, because of a family tragedy, had to leave the troupe suddenly. Desperate for a replacement, the band leader phoned Merv to ask him to fill in for the remainder of this date. Merv was more than willing to help out his one-time mentor (the solo gigs had not poured in as rapidly as had been anticipated), and made arrangements to take the next plane to the Nevada resort town.

He was followed out west by girl friend Judy Balaban, who planned to keep him company.

Not only did Merv have fun doing this final date with Martin, but there was an unexpected bonus in the trip for him also. "I'd just finished a number," he recalls, "when a six-year-old boy came up to me and said, 'We'd like to sign you for the movies.' Even for Hollywood, this talent scout seemed awfully young, so I said, 'Bug off, kid!'

"It turned out that I was talking to Terry Melcher, and he was talking for his mother, Doris Day, who was there at the hotel with her husband, Marty Melcher. Doris told me she wanted a new leading man, having become tired of being constantly cast opposite Gordon MacRae at Warner Brothers. She thought that I might be a good possibility.''

A screen test at the Burbank studio virtually assured. Merv must have spent the next few days amid fantasies of himself as the movies' greatest star. Perhaps he and Doris would even be the next Jeanette MacDonald and Nelson Eddy.

Three

Hollywood welcomed 1952 amid a climate of great trepidation. The once thriving motion picture industry was in trouble—deep trouble. Box office receipts had been steadily plummeting since their record year of 1946; theaters were folding at an alarming rate; and the product that did emerge from the major studios seldom exhibited much originality. Some "knowledgable" observers of the situation were claiming that the film industry—like the big band business—was on its last legs.

The villain of the piece was, of course, television. Although one cannot deny that the advent of this mass communications system was a major factor in toppling Hollywood from its position of authority, TV's presence served merely as the coup de grace for an industry whose foundations had already been weakened by the demise of its own ill-conceived structure.

The men who started the studios—the legendary movie moguls—had, almost without exception, begun their film careers in the exhibition end of the business. Universal's Carl Laemmle; Adolph Zukor of Paramount; William Fox, whose company would later, after a merger, become Twentieth Century-Fox; the four brothers Warner; and Louis B. Mayer and Marcus Loew of Metro-Goldwyn-Mayer—each had, at one time or another, operated a nickelodeon, owned a chain of theaters, or, simply, managed a cinema. Even the one time powerful RKO (now defunct) was a joint enterprise of the Radio Corporation of America and the Keith-Orpheum theater circuit.

Realizing that movie houses around the country needed a constant supply of product and that the *big* money could be made by *supplying* movies, rather than just exhibiting them, these pioneers (between the years 1912 and 1924) entered film production—many with a meager amount of financial backing—and, over the years, built their empires.

Once the nickelodeon disappeared in favor of the plush movie palaces that began springing up around 1914, producers readily learned that the public enjoyed going to these comfortable houses, complete with Wurlitzer organ or symphony orchestra, rather than older theaters equipped with hard seats and drab atmosphere. Indeed, with the cost of movie-making on the rise (from $500 to $1000 for a two-reel subject in 1912 to between $12,000 to $20,000 or more for a five-reel feature in 1915), the larger houses became a perfect showcase for the new product. Not only could the studios charge these exhibitors a higher fee for the pictures, but the publicity and advertising generated by the first-run engagement created a huge demand for the movies in subsequent runs in less elaborate neighborhood houses.

The exclusive, first-run playdate became vital to the success of individual pictures, and those productions that were unable to secure such engagements seldom earned a profit. To ensure the proper exposure for their films, the studios began purchasing key outlets in major cities and, failing that, building their own houses. Some independent theater owners, frightened that they might be frozen out of the competition for important pictures, decided to get into production for themselves. This was, in fact, theater chain owner Marcus Loew's primary motivation for purchasing Metro Pictures in 1920.

Another practice that infuriated theater men, but which, for years, they could do nothing about, was "block booking." As studios became all-powerful and increased their roster of stars, they would sell their entire year's product—prior to its being made—in a blind package (or block) to movie houses. Ergo, in order to get a few choice films starring Mary Pickford, Charlie Chaplin, Douglas Fairbanks, Rudolph Valentino, or some other major drawing card, owners would be forced to purchase a string of less desirable pictures—many of which were absolute turkeys. Rather than listen to pleas for fair play from the exhibitors, studios proceeded with their foul methods of distribution, forcing the more dissenting owners out of business.

Independent production companies were also having their problems. By 1920, most that owned neither booking exchanges nor theaters had ceased operations or been absorbed by a larger company.

World War I brought good fortune to the American film-makers. Because of the European conflict, almost all meaningful production ceased in England and on the Continent, making Los Angeles the motion picture capital of the world. It was well over a generation before foreign countries again assumed a truly important position in the movie industry and, during that period of hibernation, Hollywood product thrived all over the globe.

Two internal procedures which, possibly more than anything else, contributed to the growth of the studios were the "star system," coupled with the use of long-term contracts.

When the movies first began, there were no stars. Actors would work in a movie, without billing, for a few dollars per day. Producers wisely realized that players with identities would demand higher salaries. Therefore, Mary Pickford was known to her adoring public by only her screen identity of "Little Mary," and the movies' first western star, G.M. Anderson, was listed as "Broncho Billy." Other distaff performers were billed as "The Imp Girl," "The Biograph Girl," and "The Vitagraph Girl," adopting the names of their respective studios.

Carl Laemmle violated the practice of anonymity when he hired the popular Florence Lawrence away from Biograph, promising her higher wages and, most important, billing under her own name. Mary Pickford was the next player to appear under her own name, and she was followed, in short order, by matinee idols Maurice Costello and Arthur Johnson, and comedian John Bunny.

Soon, the worst fears of the producers had become a reality. Studios, in an effort to attract the stars who had the strongest drawing power with the public, began bidding against each other, offering these performers—many of whom had previously worked as truck drivers, waitresses, and even prostitutes—almost any salary which would induce them to sign with their company. The success of a studio could be measured, in no uncertain terms, by the luster of the stars it had under contract. Movies with stars made money and *good* movies with stars earned fortunes.

The coming of sound, as even the most cursory student of the cinema knows, revolutionized the industry—causing both studios and theaters to renovate their physical operations, and also forcing the retirement of some of the movies' most popular players whose voices did not match their on-screen images. The best known casualty was, of course, leading man John Gilbert.

The majors survived the talkies upheaval and, within a few years, had replenished their stables with an even more dynamic group of personalities than had graced the screen during the silent era. MGM boasted the presence of Clark Gable, Jean Harlow, Myrna Loy, Spencer Tracy, Joan Crawford, Wallace Beery, Robert Taylor, Greer Garson, and the magnificent Greta Garbo; Warners had James Cagney, Edward G. Robinson, Humphrey Bogart, Bette Davis, John Garfield, and swashbuckling Errol Flynn; at Paramount, Gary Cooper, Fredric March, Mae West, George Raft, W.C Fields, Cary Grant, Bing Crosby, and Claudette Colbert were the "money" players; Fred Astaire, Ginger Rogers, and Katharine Hepburn were at home at RKO; Tyrone Power, Alice Faye, Betty Grable, Don Ameche, Henry Fonda, Loretta Young, and cute little Shirley Temple brought in the bucks at Fox; Columbia's Harry Cohn seemed content to have discovered sultry Rita Hayworth; and over at Universal resided Deanna Durbin, Abbott and Costello, Frankenstein, Dracula, the Mummy, and the Wolf Man.

Throughout the better part of the thirties and forties, individual stars may have changed their home studios (Joan Crawford, George Raft, and Gary Cooper later made films for Warners, while Astaire and Hepburn joined the Metro roster) and others (Cary Grant) decided to free-lance, but most actors considered it advantageous to remain with a studio where they were assured a steady—and often generous—income, as well as employers who were interested in building their careers.

To protect their investments in these often unpredictable players, studios insisted they sign long-term contracts, renewable at their option every six months. Few actors bound by these agreements had any choice over the roles he or she was assigned (an exception was Warners' Paul Muni, who probably had more control of his pictures than any of his contemporaries). If the studio wanted to punish a player who'd been "naughty," it would merely assign him to an inferior film in order to teach him a lesson.

Some actors rebelled against their bondage and the most successful insurgent was Jimmy Cagney, who, whenever he felt his box office value to the studio had increased to the point where he judged he was being underpaid, would stage a walkout until Warner Brothers met his terms, which they always did.

By keeping their actors (both stars and supporting players), producers, directors, writers, and other key production personnel under these binding contracts, studios were able to hold production costs down to the point where the films could be made on comparatively (by today's standards) low budgets. If a picture went slightly over schedule, the extra cost was not nearly as great as it would be now, since most expenses were virtually controlled by almost all the crew being employees of the studio, thereby working for much less money than they would be if they'd been hired just to do the one film.

Endowed with their extensive theater ownership, the practice of block booking, dominance in the foreign marketplace, the star system, and long-term talent contracts, major studios ruthlessly controlled the motion picture industry for many decades. Then, the United States Government stepped in and the kingdom of make believe began to crumble.

Block booking aroused the ire of Congress during the mid-thirties. Independent theater owners had, indeed, captured the attention of their national representatives and, by 1936, a number of bills outlawing this studio procedure of forcing a whole year's supply upon an exhibitor were introduced.

Two years later, the Federal Government shocked the industry by filing an anti-trust suit against Paramount and seven other major studios. The Justice Department was charging combinations in restraint of trade, as well as monopoly of production, distribution, and exhibition of films, and was requesting the Court to separate studios' production and distribution activities from their theater ownership. This branch of the government had also been listening to the complaints of exhibitors.

The anti-trust trial began in New York Federal Court in 1940. Represented by an imposing staff of legal minds, the studios eventually agreed to a consent decree, which required them to sell their films in groups of five (instead of the entire season's output) and to trade screen the product in advance of selling to the exhibitor. In addition, a national arbitration system was created to deal with the complaints of theater owners.

Unfortunately for the majors, they weren't off the hook yet.

In 1946—the year of the box office bonanza—the Federal Court dealt its knockout punch to the studios. Not only was it decreed that pictures must now be sold on an *individual* basis, but the production companies were also ordered to divest themselves of their theater holdings—the operation to be completed no later than 1952. At the same time, the practice of distributor-fixed admission prices was banned.

Hollywood may have made a lot of money that year, but it also lost its basis for financial security.

Following the end of World War Two, studios found that the situation in foreign marketplaces had deteriorated as well. Pictures from England and other European countries began appearing in American theaters and, although it was a few years before these imports generated big business for distributors and exhibitors, superb efforts from Britain's J. Arthur Rank (*Hamlet, The Red Shoes*), as well as Italy's Roberto Rossellini (*Open City*) and Vittorio De Sica (*Shoeshine*), did take a share of the American recreation dollar which

71

would have otherwise gone to promote domestic productions.

Foreign governments also devised a number of restrictions and taxations in order to tie up admission revenues earned by Hollywood companies within their boundaries. Unable to return these funds to the United States, which meant a great loss of usable income for the studio, screenplays were developed for filming in these countries so that the "frozen assets" could be put to use. Metro-Goldwyn-Mayer, for example, had a small fortune in rupees tied up in India and, for this reason, produced several forgettable pictures (*Mayo, Kenner, Tarzan Goes to India*) in that country during the 1960s.

With domestic box office receipts declining during the late forties (for much the same reasons the big band business was on the downswing), the absence of the once-substantial income from foreign countries, and sufficient playdates for their product no longer a certainty, the major studios decided to make some drastic changes in their operations.

The first cutback was in the number of movies filmed each year. Without a guaranteed market for the "B" picture, it was foolish to make as many as had been produced in the past. So, with less product being turned out, there was no need to have as long a list of expensive players on salary. Actors who were sheltered by their home studios for years suddenly found themselves on the freelance market. Only those performers who had maintained their box office pull were kept on payroll, although many stars, once their contracts had expired, decided they could do financially better as an independent, and refused to resign. Now, if a studio wanted them for a specific assignment, their salary would be much higher than if they were on a weekly retainer—the new fee often including a partial ownership in the picture itself.

Whereas the studios continued to maintain long lists of contract personnel, most of these players were new, upcoming talent, whose salaries were far less than their predecessors. Only MGM carried over their impressive roster of expensive artists (Clark Gable, Spencer Tracy, Robert Taylor, Kathryn Grayson, Gene Kelly, etc.) into the mid-fifties.

Nobody in Hollywood really knew what kind of films would draw the audiences back into theaters, and an effort to discover the solution gave the public a mishmash of product, most of which was dismissed by critics and ignored by patrons. True, there were a few good original productions during this period and these, for the most part, did well. However, the bulk of what was being released was pure garbage which kept people glued to their newly purchased television sets. What was on the tube was, in general, garbage also, but at least it was free.

Considering the artistic bewilderment and weakened financial condition of the Hollywood film-makers, television veritably won the movie audience by default.

1952 found Warner Brothers struggling for survival just as desperately as the other production companies. Gone from the Burbank lot were the great, albeit costly, stars like Bogart, Bacall, Bette Davis, Robinson, Ida Lupino, John Garfield, and Ann Sheridan—all of whom had brought huge financial rewards to the studio during most of the previous two decades. Conversely, Joan Crawford was still around, as was Dennis Morgan, Ronald Reagan, Ruth Roman, Jane Wyman, Patricia Neal, Steve Cochran, and S.Z. Sakall. They had commitments to fulfill on their contract. Errol Flynn, a little worse for wear, was present also, but the remaining new films he made on the lot were uninspired, inexpensive bores.

Additionally, the studio had made a number of non-exclusive acting deals and/or signed co-production contracts with several hot, bankable stars, such as John Wayne, Randolph Scott, Gary Cooper, Burt Lancaster, and former maverick contractee, James Cagney. So successful were these arrangements that, during 1953, independent deals accounted for nearly half of Warners' output.

Many fresh faces graced the ranks of the studio's contract players—Gene Nelson, Gordon MacRae, Virginia Mayo, Frank Lovejoy, David Brian, Phyllis Thaxter, Patrice Wymore, Dick Wesson, and Virginia Gibson being the most active. If the studio was lucky, one of these fledglings would capture the fancy of the public and, as a result, achieve superstar status.

The brightest star among the newcomers was Doris Day—the cute, blond former band singer who'd discovered Merv in Las Vegas. She'd been signed by the studio during the late forties and had co-starred in such modestly-budgeted, though hit, musicals as *Romance on the High Seas, I'll See You in My Dreams, Tea for Two,* and *On Moonlight Bay.* Miss Day was, indeed, the company's most valuable property.

Despite the box office success of the actress and singer, Warners' annual contribution to the art of the cinema left much to be desired. Mediocre products like *Springfield Rifle* (Gary Cooper), *She's Working Her Way Through College* (Virginia Mayo), *This Woman is Dangerous* (Joan Crawford), *Big Jim McLain* (John Wayne), *The Crimson Pirate* (Burt Lancaster), and *Retreat, Hell!* (Frank Lovejoy) were continually fed through the studio production mill, and, whereas some of these films may have earned a few bucks, they certainly added nothing to the company's prestige, nor did they help alleviate its growing financial losses.

74

Then, during this bleak moment in the history of Warner Brothers, Mervyn burst on the scene—fresh from a successful four years as Freddy Martin's favorite male vocalist. Regrettably, he was not the panacea either.

His screen test had gone well. It consisted of a scene from John Patrick's play, *The Hasty Heart* (a Warner Brothers movie in 1949 with Ronald Reagan, Patricia Neal, and Richard Todd) and a musical number. Appearing with him in the tryout was contractee Phyllis Kirk.

"Bill Orr," reports Merv, "was so happy with what I'd done that he didn't even wait for the film to be developed, but signed me the same day as the test." Orr was a studio executive and also the son-in-law of mogul Jack Warner.

Griffin had actually gotten on Orr's good side before the test: "Bill had a reputation for never being on time, and, at our initial meeting (at which time I was supposed to sing live for him), he kept me, the casting director, and my personal manager waiting for over an hour. So, when I finally heard him coming down the hall, I ran up to the piano and sang the last few bars of 'Because,' then, pretending to leave, turned to him and asked, 'Who are you?'

"He identified himself, at which point I demanded, 'How dare you come late to my audition!' This started him laughing and, from that point, he was very receptive.

"Prior to joining Warner Brothers, incidentally, Orr had worked as an emcee in my Uncle Elmer's Sunset Strip nightclub called The Sports Circle."

The elation Merv certainly felt over his acceptance at Warners was offset somewhat by the fact that his romance with Judy Balaban had finally come to an end. Her parents, upon learning that she had gone to Las

Vegas with her singer boyfriend, panicked—thinking that the couple was going to get married—and followed her west.

"They were coming at her from all sides," Griffin recalls. "Leonard Lyons, the columnist, even spoke to both of us, advising us not to marry. I'd also heard reports that, if we *did* go ahead and wed, Barney Balaban would make it a point to 'ruin' my career in show business."

The relationship ended. Amid the deluge of pressure, Judy returned to New York, while Merv stayed in Hollywood.

Jean Barry was residing in the Los Angeles area at this time also and, one evening, the former Martin singer asked her out for dinner. "Merv needed to talk with somebody about the breakup," says Jean. "He was quite upset about it and I served as his sounding board."

Griffin did not remain in mourning for long, however, nor was he totally unhappy that the romance was over. As was the case with Gypsy Ernst, Merv felt he wasn't ready to wed yet, since, *married*, he would then have to consider his family's financial security a more important priority than the building of his career. Therefore, he might not be able to take the necessary gambles that often lead to major success. Rather than continue what had become a difficult situation, Merv decided that the honorable choice was to withdraw from the picture.

Helping him to forget Judy was a dancer named Rita Farrell, whom he'd met when both worked for Freddy Martin. The two liked each other immediately and, when Merv went out on his own, Rita became part of his act.

"Our problem," laughs Merv, "was that, in the middle of our act, we'd give each other the giggles.

"There was a time in Hartford, Connecticut, when we were doing a church benefit. I was asked to introduce the pastor, and the pianist hit a chord to get the audience's attention. Rita, thinking this was her cue, came dancing across the stage, much to everyone's surprise."

Before Merv reported to work at the studio, he and Rita finished off commitments in Reno (Mapes Hotel), Houston (the Shamrock), and Chicago (the Edgewater Beach Hotel), then set the act aside for awhile.

The performer had been signed by Warners—at three hundred dollars per week—with the idea that he would co-star with Doris Day in her next picture, *Lucky Me*. His role was to be that of a theatrical producer in his mid-thirties, but, unfortunately, in his screen test Merv photographed as if he were only nineteen. No amount of make-up could age him sufficiently. The part was eventually played by Robert Cummings.

"They also wanted me to change my name to Mark," recalls Merv, "but I'd have no part of that."

Right after he'd joined the Burbank stock company, but before the fact had been announced to the press, Merv attended a party at the home of Bill Orr, where he was introduced to Gordon MacRae—up until that time, Doris Day's most frequent leading man.

The actor and singer was very cordial to Merv, complimenting him on some of the discs he'd recorded for RCA Victor. "What are you doing in town?" he asked.

Songwriter Sammy Cahn, who was eavesdropping, couldn't resist chiming in with a jovial, "He's here to replace you, Gordon."

There was embarrassed silence and MacRae withdrew.

"That was really the only confrontation Gordon and I had," remembers Griffin, "yet the fan magazines and gossip columnists started claiming that we were feuding. Not true!"

Rather than give their new actor dramatic lessons ("They told me they didn't want me to change a bit and to stay away from acting coaches"), the studio decided to let him have some practical experience, assigning him a small role in *Cattle Town*, a low budget, black-and-white western, released in 1952. Noel Smith directed (for producer Bryan Foy) the trite screenplay by Tom Blackburn, which featured a cast headed by Dennis Morgan, Philip Carey, Amanda Blake, and Rita Moreno. Billed twelfth, Merv had the part of "Joseph," secretary to the Governor of Texas.

"In my first scene," he says, "I was to enter and announce, 'The governor wants to see Shiloh,' then open the door and exit. The first part went fine, but when I grabbed the door handle to leave, it came off in my hand."

His next picture was *By the Light of the Silvery Moon* (1953), a nostalgic Technicolor adapation of Booth Tarkington's Penrod stories, and a sequel to the earlier *On Moonlight Bay*. Produced by William Jacobs, it was directed by David Butler, from a script by Robert O'Brien and Irving Elinson.

"I was thrilled when they called me to work on it," Griffin recalls. "Doris Day was top-billed, and I thought, 'At last—our picture together.' I should have suspected something was wrong when I learned they'd been shooting for a couple of weeks already. On the way to the set, I ran into Gordon MacRae and wondered, 'What's he doing in my picture?' I hung around all day before the director called me. Finally, when my time came, I found I had only one line in the whole thing! It was an ice-skating scene near the end, and I, in a mackinaw, had to announce: 'All you figure skaters grab your favorite partner and let's skate to our favorite song!' Then they played 'By the Light of the Silvery Moon.' MacRae, of course, had the male lead.''

Besides Miss Day and MacRae, the musical comedy featured Leon Ames, Rosemary DeCamp, Mary Wickes, and Billy Gray. Merv did *not* receive billing.

''Having such an inconsequential part was, naturally, disappointing,' he says, ''but, every time I'd see Doris on the lot, she'd promise that she would try to get me a break soon.''

That break came with Merv's next picture.

Warners had obtained the rights to the story of late opera and film star Grace Moore and approached MGM contractee Kathryn Grayson to play the title role. As she recalls: ''The script was so good that I obtained my release from Metro in order to do this picture; then, after I'd signed for the part, Moore's widower withdrew permission to have himself dramatized in the movie. This meant that the script had to be re-written and a lot of extra songs were added to fill in the eliminated scenes.''

The musical was entitled *So This Is Love*. Billed *second* in the Gordon Douglas-directed/Henry Blanke-produced movie, based on a screenplay by John Monks, Jr., was Merv Griffin, who played Buddy Nash, the actor-manager fiancé of the star. Although his role lasted only fifteen minutes (he married someone else when Moore ignored him in favor of her career), Merv did get to sing a number, ''I Kiss Your Hand. Madame.''

Kathryn Grayson: ''I first met Merv when we pre-recorded the musical numbers. Unlike many actors, he had no ego problems and was such a nice guy that I thought to myself, 'He'll never go anyplace in this business.' ''

While making this picture, Merv began to give second thoughts to the idea of being a movie star: ''I was doing

79

an intimate love scene with Miss Grayson one day when the entire University of Texas football team, in California for a game, trooped into the studio and stood around watching me try to make love to her. I was petrified with embarrassment.

"Kathryn was very gracious to me on that picture. There were a couple of times when she would ruin her own take in order to maneuver me into a better position, whispering, 'How are you ever going to be a star if you don't turn your face toward the camera.' "

Reviews on the Technicolor production were fairly good, with the bulk of the top notices going to the female star. Merv was mentioned in many of the critiques, but none of the comments were anything to get excited about.

Since he was under contract, the studio sent their young actor out on a national tour to promote *So This Is Love*. Trips of this sort can be back-breaking experiences—a half dozen interviews every day, with each one having to sound like it's absolutely fresh—but Griffin, who'd spent the better part of four years on a band bus, found this traveling easy by comparison.

When he arrived in Detroit, Merv found that ex-boss Freddy Martin was appearing at a local nightclub, so, after the last show, he invited the leader and his entire company up to his hotel suite, threw them a lavish reunion party, and let all the guys in the band phone their wives in California—then charged the whole thing to Warner Brothers.

At the conclusion of his thirty day, twenty-seven city tour, Merv returned to San Mateo where one hundred persons jammed the Skyroom of that city's Villa Chartier for a dinner in his honor. During his talk to the group, the actor expressed his ambition to someday set up a scholarship to aid talented San Mateo youths in building careers in show business. "After all," he said, "the only place to get a real break is in New York or Hollywood. If these young people could get to those cities, it would bring many of them good careers."

All over the room, people rose to pledge huge amounts of money to the project. ("Up jumped my father, who shouted he'd be in charge of the money. Everybody roared.")

"I'll never forget the press screening of *So This Is Love*," muses Griffin. "It was held at the Hollywood Pantages Theater. When I came on the screen, I, literally, slid on the floor and Rita, who was with me, got the giggles. Afterwards, out in the lobby, Hedda Hopper came up to me, gave me a hug, and said, 'You were magnificent. You're going to be a big star.'

"Unfortunately, the movie didn't do too well. It opened the day after Cinemoscope came out and there we were, stuck up on that postage stamp when everyone was talking about 'wide screen.' "

The studio brass didn't really approve of Merv's being seen in public with an unknown like Rita Farrell and insisted that he go to premieres with other startlets whose names connected with his would make good items for the gossip columns. Griffin, who was smitten with the dancer, cooperated in this area . . . only up to a point: "I'd usually take Dolores Dorn-Heft to the premieres. We'd arrive in a limousine . . . be interviewed by Larry Finley in front of the theater about how we were looking forward to seeing this fantastic new movie . . . then walk inside, and immediately go our separate ways out the side door. Rita would be waiting in a car for me and Dolores' date would be there also. We never stayed for those movies . . . just went for the publicity."

When Rita was not in town, Merv would go out with others. He once had a date with Gloria DeHaven and, upon arriving at her door, found tall, heroic John

Payne, the actress' estranged husband, there looming over him. Lightweight, non-physical Griffin, who would have been no match for Payne even with one of the latter's hands tied behind his back, had a few anxious seconds, trying to judge whether the larger man was planning to give him the bum's rush.

"Come on in, kid," Payne said, finally flashing a friendly smile. "Gloria's getting dressed and I'm here to baby-sit."

On another occasion, Merv and actress Marilyn Erskine (*The Eddie Cantor Story*) were doubling with newlyweds Tony Curtis and Janet Leigh, enroute to Jerry Lewis' Halloween party. Both couples were in costume. Tony was dressed as Janet and vice versa, while Griffin and Erskine were dressed as the characters played by Shirley Booth and Burt Lancaster in *Come Back, Little Sheba*. The rub was that Merv was disguised in Miss Booth's slovenly robe and Marilyn had on Lancaster's duds.

It wasn't until the motorcycle cop pulled their car over that the fun *really* began. Curtis certainly had one hell of a time explaining the reasons for his wearing long blond curls.

There was one beautiful starlet Merv occasionally dated who had a mother he couldn't stand. The older woman did not like him, either.

The feud, it seems, started over Mom's two French poodles, who were continually smelling up the actor's automobile. "I think she fed them a steady diet of beans," he says. "I finally just kicked her out of the car."

Since he was still going out with the daughter, Griffin and Mom were forced into each other's company from time to time. Ignoring her curt attitude, Merv, who was not one to be intimidated by anyone— especially after his experience with the Hazel Bishop representative—would arrive at the door, greet the woman with something like "Hi, Mom. How's your ass?" grab his girl and depart, leaving the woman mumbling to herself about "indecencies" as she watched them drive off.

At the studio Merv was kept busy between acting assignments "donating" his voice to films in which he did not actually appear. "I was America's favorite voice-over," he quips. Indeed, astute viewers of the late show can catch Merv's golden tones as a voice on the telephone in Alfred Hitchcock's thriller, *I Confess*, and as a radio announcer ("Well, folks, here's another one of those silly reports about sea serpents again") in *The Beast from 20,000 Fathoms*.

"I had even more to do," reports Merv, "in a 3-D western with Guy Madison, called *The Charge at Feather River*. There was a death scene by a Polish actor that had to be re-dubbed. When the studio got around to it, the actor who'd played the part on the screen was in Europe, so I was elected to re-do his entire death scene."

Griffin's next acting job in front of the cameras was quite a comedown from the important role he'd played in *So This Is Love*. The film was *Three Sailors and a Girl*, a light, breezy Technicolor musical starring Jane Powell, Gordon MacRae, Gene Nelson, Sam Levene, and Jack E. Leonard. Songwriter Sammy Cahn produced the Roland Kibbee/Devery Freeman screenplay, which was directed by Roy Del Ruth. The script was, in truth, based on a 1925 play by George S. Kaufman, *The Butter and Egg Man*—filmed four times previously by Warners (under the original title with Jack Mulhall in 1928; as *The Tenderfoot* with Joe E. Brown in 1932; *Dance, Charlie, Dance* with Stuart Erwin in 1937; and as *An Angel From Texas* with Eddie Albert in 1940).

The story of the 1953 release concerned three sailors (MacRae, Nelson, and Leonard), and how they invest their shipmates' back pay ($50,000) in a Broadway musical, starring Miss Powell and produced by the fast-talking Levene. Playing themselves in cameo roles were director George Abbott, playwright Moss Hart, and composer Ira Gershwin. Burt Lancaster was also around for a gag appearance at the finish.

Merv's unbilled part? He played one of the sailors on the submarine who gave the stars his money to invest. Aside from an occasional brief line of dialogue, all he really did was decorate the background: "I spent the whole picture standing behind Jack E. Leonard, who was in his really fat days then. All through the movie it looked like Jack had a wart on his head—me!"

Merv recalls that Leonard, who had it written into his contract that, at lunch, he was to be driven via limousine to the commissary (fifty feet away from the sound stage), was constantly breaking him up during the film. "There was a scene where I get angry at Gordon and make a lunge toward him, but Jack stops me. I did the bit, then started laughing. The director didn't notice I'd broken concentration and yelled 'That's a print!' Unfortunately, nobody saw what I'd done until after a couple screenings of the rushes and the set had been broken down. It would have cost too much to re-shoot the scene, so the flub is still in the picture. Sammy Cahn was furious."

Merv's personal manager at this point in his career was one George "Bullets" Durgom, a short, colorful man, who was (and still is) considered by many to be one of the most astute artists' representatives in the entertainment industry. For years, his top client was Jackie Gleason.

Durgom had first met Griffin when he had stopped by the Coconut Grove one evening to listen to Freddy

Martin. Since he was accompanied by the lovely Lana Turner, Merv had made it a point to approach the table during intermission, where the two men became acquainted. Bullets was partially responsible some time later for convincing Merv that he should leave Freddy and strike out on his own—with himself as the young singer's manager.

Not satisfied with the parts his client was getting at Warners, Durgom scouted around the other studios to see if he could find a choice assignment there for Merv. At Paramount, there was an excellent singing role in a western musical fantasy, entitled *Red Garters*. Rosemary Clooney and Jack Carson had already been set for the leads, but this other male part was prime . . . and, more important, the producer was interested in Griffin. Sadly, Barney Balaban still had the final word at that studio and, once he heard that our hero was under consideration, that was that.

Another role Bullets tried to get for Merv was that of Ensign Willie Keith in *The Caine Mutiny*, which Stanley Kramer was producing at Columbia. After insisting that he wear lifts, Durgom dragged his client over to the studio on Gower to see casting director Max Arno. Barging into the executive's office, Durgom announced, "Max, here's your Willie Keefer."

"Who's Willie Keefer?" was the reply.

Obviously, the manager had gotten his character names mixed up. He corrected himself, but it didn't make any difference. Willie Keith was eventually played by Robert Francis, while the Keefer assignment went to Fred MacMurray.

Merv found the Hollywood routine a welcome change from life on Freddy Martin's bus. He'd rented a furnished house from his manager at $125 per month and, with his pleasing personality, was making friends quickly. "Of course, as I look back on it now," he admits, "it was just the comparison with being on the road that made my life during 1952-54 seem so settled down."

The studio was, actually, keeping him quite busy with an occasional role, voice-overs, and publicity sessions. Yet, Merv also was beginning to realize that film-making was a dull process—sitting around the set for hours while waiting to be called for a scene: "I had thought it would be fun to be a movie star. I didn't know you had to act. I missed the audience—getting a reaction after I finished—and was, frankly, bored."

If Merv had any second thoughts about his wanting to quit being a film star, they were certainly dismissed after his next movie, a color western entitled *The Boy From Oklahoma* (1954), and starring Will Rogers, Jr., Nancy Olson, and Lon Chaney. Michael Curtiz (*Casablanca, Yankee Doodle Dandy*) directed the Frank Davis/Winston Miller screenplay, with David Weisbart its producer. Griffin, playing Rogers' deputy sheriff in this tired little effort, had seventh billing.

"I'd never been on a horse before," says Merv, "and Mike Curtiz promised me two weeks of instruction before we began filming. But, he double-crossed me.

"I was called to the set the first day of shooting and told to *lead* a fifty-man posse—all experienced riders—down a hill. My protests fell on deaf ears.

"There I was coming down the hill at a gallop, holding the reins with one hand, and frantically keeping my hat from slipping off with other. Suddenly, I realized the posse had passed me.

"Curtiz yelled, 'Cut!' then looked at me and said, 'Greefing, you stink on de lousy horse!'

"All through the picture it was the same way. I'd fall off my horse, my hat kept slipping down over my eyes, and I blinked everytime I shot a gun."

In one scene, Griffin decided to have some fun and,

after making his scripted announcement ("Come on, everybody. Clear the street for the horse race!"), did an impression (physically only) of Jackie Gleason's famous "Away we go" exit. Curtiz, who didn't watch Gleason's show and, therefore, was unaware of why the cast and crew were laughing, decided to leave this 1954 gag in the 1800s western.

"Mike Curtiz was quite a character," recalls Griffin. "I ran into him one morning and he was in tears—completely broken up. I asked him what was wrong, and he said, 'Greefing, I've been at Warner Brothers twenty years. Jack Warner just walked by me and didn't say, "Good morning." ' "

A few weeks later, Merv was driving down Sunset Boulevard, when he spotted the director in the next car with a sultry blond (obviously not his wife) beside him. "Hiya, Mike," he said, grinning from ear to ear. Startled at being discovered in this suspicious situation, Curtiz pressed down on the accelerator, driving off the boulevard and onto somebody's front lawn.

Griffin, soured by his experience in *The Boy From Oklahoma*, became camera shy and started to duck the casting office. "Whenever they would call," he explains, "I used to answer the telephone in my Chinese voice. I'd say 'Mastah Griffin no here, he in San Diego.' "

Nevertheless, Warners was able to coerce him into one final assignment—an adaptation by Harold Medford and James R. Webb of Edgar Allen Poe's *Murders in the Rue Morgue*. The studio had had a tremendous success in 1953 with their 3-D color production of *House of Wax*, featuring Vincent Price, and, now, in 1954, decided to do another 3-D horror production (utilizing many sets from the earlier effort), entitled *Phantom of the Rue Morgue*. The stars of this mediocre film were Karl Malden, Claude Dauphin,

Patricia Medina, and Steve Forrest, with direction by Roy Del Ruth.

Merv's part was that of a French student at the Sorbonne ("With this Irish puss!"), who, for a brief time, is a suspect in the series of brutal murders.

Although he never really went out of his way to see that Merv got bigger and better roles (in all fairness, because of Merv's very youthful countenance, he was difficult to cast), studio head Jack Warner liked Griffin and often included him on the guest list of his private parties.

For the first affair he attended at the "Colonel's" mansion, Merv was advised to bring a date with a "title," since the all-powerful host liked to mix with "royalty." After giving the matter some thought, Merv invited Lorraine Manville, niece of the much-married millionaire, Tommy Manville. Lorraine just happened to be the Countess Lorraine du Monceau.

When they arrived at the formal dinner, the couple spotted their host dancing at the other end of the ballroom. Warner saw them also, came over, gave Merv a firm handshake, and said, "Hiya, Griff!" Then, following an introduction to the actor's date, the studio chief replied, "Hiya, Countess. I want you to meet Princess Ali Kahn."

He was, of course, referring to the gorgeous Rita Hayworth, his dancing parther.

More introductions followed and, as Merv recollects, "My girl had the lowest ranking title in the room. There was one Queen Mother and many princesses."

At the conclusion of dinner, Warner made a toast to the royalty in the form of a poem. At its finish, he seemed to be stuck for a final rhyming line. Quick-thinking Merv supplied the verse, a gesture which put him in solid with his boss.

"When the speech was finished," recalls Merv,

"Warner, employing his usual 'good taste,' announced, 'Now, we men are going to sit here and have our cigars, so why don't you ladies go and take a piss!' "

Griffin, at later functions in the Warner home, became more or less a troubleshooter for the Colonel. After each of Jack's grand dinners, which were attended by everyone from the Michael Wildings (Elizabeth Taylor) to the Robert Taylors (Ursula Thiess), the top talents in Hollywood (such as Judy Garland and Doris Day) got up and entertained. "One night," remembers Merv, "it was Mimi Benzell who performed, singing seventeen songs that nobody had ever heard of. Jack said to me, 'Get her off, damn it, Griffin.'

"She asked if anyone wanted to hear anything else. I said, 'Do you know "Tippy Tippy Tin?" ' Everyone laughed. That was how I got her off."

While in tinsel-town, Merv was also a partygiver, regularly hosting an informal gathering every Sunday afternoon for friends like the Aldo Rays and the Tony Curtises. The get-togethers were reminiscent of the Sundays of Merv's youth in San Mateo, with the whole gang standing around the piano after dinner to sing their favorite tunes.

Uncle Elmer Griffin, still a Los Angeles resident, would often join the group. One Sunday that the tennis champ was present, who should unexpectedly appear at the door, but Jack Warner.

"Everyone was quite surprised and, frankly, somewhat intimidated when he first arrived," says Merv, "but Jack quickly put them at ease and even got up at the piano and sang 'Tea for Two.' Then he saw Elmer and asked, 'What does your fat uncle do?''

" 'My Uncle Elmer is in real estate,' I said, 'but he's also a fine tennis player.' "

Warner, who prided himself on his tennis game, ordered: "Well, bring him over to my house next

Sunday. He and Bill Orr can play Solly Biano and myself." Biano was the studio casting director.

Griffin knew very well that *nobody* beat Jack Warner . . . not if they wanted to stay on his payroll, but since the performer really wanted out of his contract, he told his uncle that, under no circumstances should he do anything but defeat the studio head six-love, which, of course, Elmer did without any trouble whatsoever.

"Warner was furious," laughs Merv. "He cursed like hell . . . threw his racket across the court."

After that fateful tennis match, Griffin knew that his days at the studio were numbered. Most of the other contractees had been released from their bonds (the majority of pictures now carrying the Warner shield were being made independently), and, as he recalls, "Doris Day and I were the only ones left."

Finally, to end the waiting, Griffin went up to Warner's office for a showdown.

"I'd like out of my contract," he informed his boss.

"Somebody else want to sign you?" was the immediate response. "Or do you just want more money?"

Merv explains: "I didn't want more money, I just wanted out. I wanted to play before live audiences again. So, Jack said, 'All right, five thousand and you're out.'

"I gave him the check and promised I wouldn't work in Hollywood for two years. Then, he tore up the check, saying, 'If you do another movie within two years, I'll be very disappointed in you.'

" 'I'm not even staying in Hollywood,' I announced. 'I'm going back to New York.' "

Griffin's less-than-successful career as a movie star had come to an end. The time he'd spent in Hollywood had, from a practical standpoint, been a waste, since it cost him the momentum he had going for himself when he'd left Martin in 1952.

His recording career with RCA Victor had, for the most part, fizzled also. True, he'd cut an excellent disc with "Once in Love with Amy," but almost immediately after, Ray Bolger had come out with *his* version of the same song, and Merv's quickly vanished from the charts.

His other promising recording was a piece called "The Morning Side of the Mountain," however, the company's promotion department made up a demo disc for radio stations with the tune backed by one from Eddie Fisher, entitled "Wish You Were Here," and history tells us which number got the most air play.

In retrospect, Merv feels that part of his unhappiness during the Hollywood period of his life had something to do with his having lost his excess poundage some years before. "I almost became blasé. I began to look in the mirror and think of myself as a leading man. This was a ridiculous state for me and contrary to my whole attitude. The fat boy suddenly becomes vain. You can see how silly it was. I realized this and began to resist it.

"We once thought it might be funny to devote one of the talk shows to a 'Merv Griffin Film Festival,' yet, after we looked at all the clips, realized that the whole thing would last four minutes."

Not one to dwell on failure, Griffin began making plans to regain the ground he'd lost while at Warners. He knew that the place to start the career going again would be in New York, but before he headed for the east coast, he had a date to keep in Las Vegas—with one of the most fascinating personalities in all of show business.

Four

Stylish, yet earthy, witty and unpredictable are four choice adjectives which partially describe the sultry, gravel-voiced Tallulah Bankhead, who, among her other accomplishments, made "dahling" a household word. This tempestuous star of plays like *The Little Foxes, The Skin of Our Teeth,* and *Private Lives,* as well as Alfred Hitchcock's taut one-set screen thriller, *Lifeboat,* not only captured the attention of New York theater audiences with her highly individualized performances (her contribution to the Broadway production of *Antony and Cleopatra* received the classic critical comment, "Tallulah Bankhead barged down the Nile last night as Cleopatra—and sank"), but also the nation's headlines as a result of her often outrageous escapades ("I don't care what they say as long as they talk about me").

Merv Griffin had first worked with the colorful lady on her NBC radio variety program, "The Big Show," reportedly budgeted at fifty thousand dollars per week. Then, right after his release from Warners, he received an offer to appear on the bill with her at the Sands Hotel in Las Vegas. He accepted immediately, knowing this would be a perfect opportunity to re-establish himself in the variety field.

Tallulah was fifty-two when the twenty-nine-year-old Griffin was selected to open her Vegas act—doing a casual twenty minutes of listenable songs. Recently having undergone a mammoplasty, she, at one of their initial meetings, seized the opportunity to reveal her beautiful new breasts, with the explanation, "It's not plastic, you know, dahling. It's me!"

Merv, like most who knew Tallulah, was at a loss for words.

Written by Goodman Ace, Bankhead's act, a series of songs, impersonations, and readings from Dorothy Parker, was a good one, drawing a big money crowd. As Merv recalls, "Tallulah loved the Vegas underworld . . . the 'Louies' and the 'Leftys.' She found them to be fascinating characters."

She also liked Merv . . . trusted him, and, during the period they worked together, kept bugging him to escort her across the street, so she could see Bobby Short perform at another hotel. "Finally, I agreed," says Griffin. "We went there and Tallulah laughed unroariously at the comic who opened the show, but, when it was Short's turn, she began talking very loud and continued to do so through his entire act.

" 'What is this, Tallulah,' I said. 'You've been after me for two weeks to take you to see Bobby Short, and now you don't even listen to him.'

" 'Nonsense, dahling,' she answered. 'I heard every word he said.' "

Following a short bout with laryngitis which caused Merv to miss the second night of the engagement, he found that the star was giving him the silent treatment. He confronted her and she explained: "You son-of-a-bitch. You know I can't stand when other people are sick. Immediately, I think I have it. If I'm around a stutterer, I stammer. If I hear about an automobile accident, I feel bruised."

"What happens if you hear about rape," asked Griffin.

"I masturbate, dahling," she laughingly replied.

Merv will never forget his closing night at the Sands. "At the party, Tallulah ordered a zombie and so did I.

It was like fruit punch—nothing happened. So we changed to daiquiris. We were both dead drunk, and dead drunk we played blackjack—which was strictly against the house rules at the Sands. Entertainers appearing there were not allowed to gamble at the hotel's casino.

"We stayed at the table all night, and by ten the next morning—with guests in their bathing suits gathered around to watch—I'd won twelve thousand, and Tallulah had eight.

"Jack Entratter, entertainment director and part owner of the hotel, came over—and was he angry. He took both of us firmly by the arms, cashed in our chips, and led us upstairs while the crowd watched in stunned silence—waiting for Tallulah's exit line, which everyone knew was inevitable.

"Halfway up the stairs, she turned back to her public and said, 'Well, isn't anyone going to fuck me tonight, dahling?' Everybody broke up—including Entratter."

(Merv recalls that Miss Bankhead's final television appearance, several years later, was on his talk show for Westinghouse. "Margaret Truman was on the program also and, at one point, the former President's daughter admitted that she was forty-two years old. 'Please, dahling,' said Tallulah, 'people may be eating!' ")

With his Vegas winnings secure in his pocket, Merv, accompanied by girl friend Rita Farrell, proceeded to drive back east to the hustling city of New York. However, in Harrisburg, Pennsylvania, he had problems. His new Ford cracked the block and, when the local dealer began giving him a hard time, the entertainer picked up the phone to call his friend Edsel Ford direct. He'd met the auto executive a couple of months earlier while playing in an industrial show for the company.

The local Ford dealer couldn't believe his ears when

Edsel commanded, "Give Mr. Griffin a brand new motor."

Although he'd made up his mind that he didn't really want to devote his life to a singing career ("After losing my voice that time in Vegas, I decided it was stupid for one to count on their singing voice in order to make a living"), Merv did spend the summer of 1954 crooning over CBS in a series of twice-weekly musical telecasts. He and Betty Ann Grove were, in fact, replacing such highpriced luminaries as Dinah Shore, Perry Como, Jo Stafford, and Jane Froman, who did these spots during the winter months.

In the fall, Griffin hit the road again, appearing in nightclubs and hotels around the country. Then, he returned to New York, resolving that he was through singing other people's words. "It was the worst slump of my career. I told my agent that I wanted to be an emcee and that I'd only sing if I got the 'talking' jobs also.

"In any slump, you begin to question yourself and your talents. You find you're trying to prove yourself to your agents. I knew I could handle an emceeing assignment if I could only get a chance. Maybe it was ego or something, but I knew.

"Actually, I was getting some experience doing interviews even then. Barry Gray used to do a local radio show from a Manhattan restaurant—chatting with celebrities—and, on his nights off, I'd substitute for him."

Merv reports that he only worked four weeks in 1955—in a revival of the E.Y. Harburg/Fred Saidy/Burton Lane musical-comedy, *Finian's Rainbow*, at the New York City Center. His salary was a paltry eight-five dollars per week (Merv borrowed money from his manager to make ends meet), but he felt that his participation in this production might lead to something better. "A time like this is when prayer comes in. You just keep praying and keep working."

Griffin readily admits that he had absolutely no discipline for Broadway and, as a consequence, was constantly in conflict with the orchestra conductor of *Finian's*—Julius Rudel: "It was my fault because I sang the songs with the same relaxed phrasing that I'd used in a nightclub, or on records, which is not the way of the theater. On opening night, I did 'Old Devil Moon' like Sinatra. Rudel came backstage after the performance and was furious with me. He had every right to be."

Merv's performance as the show's romantic hero, Woody Mahoney, received little more than polite notice from the critics. Probably the best comment came from John McLain of the *Journal-American*, who called him "an assured and prepossessing performer with a good voice."

Aside from his spats with the conductor, Merv also feuded with Helen Gallagher, the production's leading lady: "I was standing in the wings one night, waiting to follow Helen on stage. Just before she entered, she gave me a tremendous punch in the stomach, which knocked my wind out. I followed her on—in tremendous pain—and, almost immediately, had to sing my big number, 'Old Devil Moon.'

"As I sang, locked in an embrace with her, she reached up and grabbed the back of my head by the short hairs. I had to go on as if nothing had happened.

"Then, it was her turn to sing a verse, and I squeezed her as tight as I could so that she couldn't make a sound. Rudel had to hold the note with the orchestra and the audience didn't know what was happening, but Helen never gave me a bad time again."

Finian's Rainbow was not the only occasion when Merv had a problem with his improper phrasing. Manager Durgom had secured for him an audition with

MERV

Merv and author Michael B. Druxman on "The Merv Griffin Show" talk about the biography, **Merv.** Merv was an extremely cooperative subject, and he loved the book when it was first published in 1976. *Michael B. Druxman*

Merv Griffin at the start of his career.
Pictorial Parade.

Freddy Martin and Merv Griffin. In the late 40s and early 50s Merv was "the boy singer" in Freddy Martin's band, a celebrated spot for any young man.
Pictorial Parade.

Merv Griffin, Columbia recording artist, playing his new hit song for teenagers at a publicity party in Kansas City.
Pictorial Parade

Four top crooners of the 40's and 50's, Perry Como, Vic Damone, Eddie Fisher and Merv Griffin, harmonizing for the camera.
Popsie, Pictorial Parade.

Merv Griffin on a cross-country promotional tour for Warner
Brothers.
Pictorial Parade.

Kathryn Grayson and Merv Griffin as they appeared in their leading roles in the 1953 film **So This Is Love.**
The Doug McClelland Collection

In 1954 Merv Griffin (L) starred in the Warner Brothers film **The Boy From Oklahoma.** His co-stars were William Zuckert, Sheb Wooley, Louis Jean Heydt and Will Rogers, Jr.
The Doug McClelland Collection

Merv Griffin, his wife Julann and son Tony at their 20-acre Califon, New Jersey home.
The Doug McClelland Collection

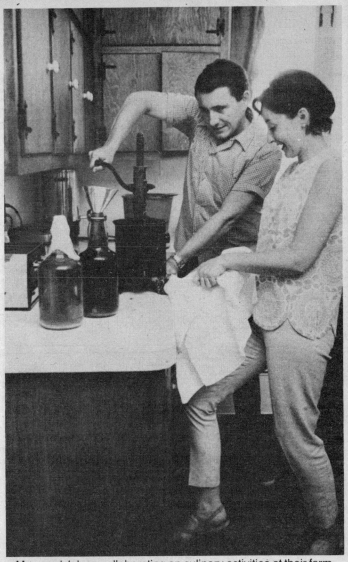

Merv and Julann collaborating on culinary activities at their farm, Teetertown.
Globe Photos

ABOVE: Merv and his son, Anthony Patrick Griffin, born December 8, 1959, the same day that Merv debuted as game show host of "Play Your Hunch" on NBC.
Globe Photos

RIGHT: Merv Griffin on the air.
The Doug McClelland Collection

ABOVE: Merv Griffin with his long-time sidekick, Arthur Treacher, in 1967. The British-born performer was famous as the screen's "perfect butler" during the 30's and 40's in Hollywood.
UPI

LEFT: Merv Griffin and his musical director Mort Lindsey in 1970.
The Doug McClelland Collection

ABOVE: Merv Griffin with Jack Sheldon, singer, comedian and first trumpet with the Mort Lindsey Orchestra on "The Merv Griffin Show."
The Doug McClelland Collection

RIGHT: Merv steps onto the Hollywood Palace stage at showtime of his TV show.
The Doug McClelland Collection

Merv and Julann Griffin attend a party at the "Bistro."
Eventually, they divorced.
Frank Edwards, Fotos International

Merv, accompanied by his son, Tony, achieved the mark of success when Merv was awarded a "star" on Hollywood Boulevard.
Nate Cutler, Globe Photos

Merv, an avid tennis player, always fond of fresh air and exercise, used to consider himself an eternal dieter.
Globe Photos

Merv Griffin today. Still handsome, witty, and unpretentious, to this day doesn't consider himself a star.
The Doug McClelland Collection

Merv with his son, Tony, who now realizes show business is a business, which he's studying. He heads a musical group called Karma Rock.
Nate Cutler, Globe Photos

Richard Rodgers and Oscar Hammerstein II for the role of "Prince Charming" in their television production of *Cinderella*: 'I went in, sang 'It Might as Well Be Spring,' and halfway through the number, Rodgers stopped me with, 'Mr. Griffin, I don't recall writing the song that way.'

" 'That's the way it's sung on records,' I explained, not realizing he wanted a more formal phrasing.

" 'I didn't write it for *records*, Mr. Griffin,' he said, 'I wrote it for motion pictures.' "

Merv did not get the part.

Another television special Griffin almost auditioned for was Max Liebman's production of *The Desert Song*: "I knew I was all wrong for the leading part in this show, but Bullets insisted that I go in and see the producer, again wearing lifts. The first thing Liebman said to me was, 'Why are you walking so funny?'

"I explained I had on elevator shoes and that, frankly, I wasn't right for the role. Afterwards, when I didn't get it, Bullets was so angry, he told me I'd ruined my chances for an important show business career."

If nothing else happened during this period, Merv had gained a reputation as being the best *utility* singer in New York: "Whenever a producer needed a singer fast, they'd say, 'Get Merv! He can make all our props look good.'

"Their favorite device was to use me in a beach number. I was always singing behind an umbrella or a water fall."

Finally forced to do straight singing appearances on television in order to eat, Merv had been able to secure a couple of spots on the always popular "Jackie Gleason Show." The funnyman just happened to be a client of Bullets Durgom also.

Griffin enjoyed the shows with Jackie, although, on one occasion, the overweight comedian insisted he sing the words to the program's theme song—"Melancholy Serenade"—then rewrote the lyrics thirty minutes before airtime.

He was also a featured vocalist on one of Kate Smith's earlier television programs, sponsored by Esquire Boot Polish: "They pulled me off the show when they realized my name was Griffin." (Coincidentally, Griffin Shoe Polish would later sponsor Merv's program, "Play Your Hunch.")

Finally, Merv got his opportunity to do more than just sing when he accepted the emcee job in the summer of 1955 for the CBS Sunday morning religious-jazz program, "Look Up and Live." The position paid a mere $119 per week, but it did offer the aspiring host good training in this area. He was introducing pastors, gospel singers like Mahalia Jackson, and setting the scene for dramatic presentations.

An occasional actor on the show was Sidney Poitier, who, at this time, operated a drama school in Harlem. Merv recalls a conversation he had with Poitier over breakfast one morning. "He asked me what I would do if I couldn't get another job in show business when this one finally dried up, and, after thinking for a moment, I said that it might be fun to be an agent.

"I didn't see Sidney again for several years, until after he'd become a major star. We ran into each other in Sardi's. I asked him, 'Do you still have your drama school?' and he smiled and answered, 'No. Are you still an agent?' "

Sadly, Merv's job on the CBS show lasted only thirteen weeks. "The program was under Protestant supervision. After a time, it was the turn of the Catholics to run the series. As soon as the Catholics came on, they dropped me. I said, 'You can't do that; I'm a Catholic.' But they dropped me fast."

The following year, CBS tapped Merv to both sing

and talk to "The Morning Show"—that network's answer to NBC's popular eye-opener, "Today." John Henry Falk, who later made history in a sensational lawsuit dealing with blacklisting (*Fear on Trial*), was host when Merv joined the program, but he was later replaced by Dick Van Dyke. "Dick was so nervous the day before his first show," recalls Merv, "that he stayed up late that night and overslept—missing the program altogether. I was, therefore, chosen to substitute and they told me that if I got stuck for something to say, I should read one of the many public service spots which dealt with the prevention of one disease or another."

Griffin was on "The Morning Show" for about six months, leaving when hosting chores were assumed by Will Rogers, Jr. After that, he received a bid from producer Martin Stone, to take over Bob Smith's job on the highly successful children's show, "Howdy Doody." (Smith, at that time, was laid up due to a heart attack.) Not wanting to play second fiddle to a puppet, Merv declined the offer and looked around for a job with more promise to it.

Irving Mansfield, who'd produced the summer replacement series Merv'd done with Betty Ann Grove and was now doing similar chores for bespectacled radio and television comedian Robert Q. Lewis, came to his rescue—temporarily. Upon learning Merv was out of work, Mansfield approached Lewis with the suggestion that they use Griffin to replace their juvenile singer, Richard Hayes, recently drafted. Bob met the "bright and pudgy" young man and agreed.

Lewis' variety program aired live over the CBS television network every morning for a half hour, Monday through Friday, as well as on Saturday morning radio. His regulars included Ray Block and his orchestra, Jaye P. Morgan, the singing team of Lois Hunt and Earl Wrightson, a group, the Chordettes, announcer Lee Vines, and a perky young comedienne named Julann Wright. Merv joined the company at a salary of five hundred per week.

Robert Q. Lewis recalls those hectic days of live television, when he was required to present a fresh, funny show six days per week. "We were always looking for new material that we could use, and, therefore, a writer was not measured by the quality of his work, but the quantity. If a new writer came in with pages, we didn't read the stuff—we weighed it.

"Every day, we had to do a mini-revue. I'd do a monologue; there'd be a comedy sketch; three or four songs; and, finally, a production number. It was really a backbreaking chore to get the show on."

Among the then-unknown writers who worked briefly for Lewis on this program were Paddy Chayefsky, George Axelrod, and Neil Simon.

Lewis' show was in the same vogue as the formats for which Jack Benny and Arthur Godfrey were famous, in that the host would be surrounded by a "family." Each had a boy and girl singer, a band leader, an announcer (Vines' on camera personality, for example, was that of a ladies' man), and a scatterbrain secretary. Filling this last slot for Lewis was Miss Julann Elizabeth Wright, who doubled as the star's off-camera secretary.

Born on January 30, 1929, in Ironwood, Michigan—a logging and mining town which boasted a population then of sixteen thousand (including hermits)—Miss Wright grew up "losing myself in characterizations and dreaming of becoming a great actress." With the blessings of her parents (her father was a judge), she went off to join a stock company in Roanoake, Virginia, then journeyed to New York where she obtained a role in the off-Broadway production of *Teach Me How to Cry*.

Robert Q. Lewis initially hired her as his part-time

secretary because he liked the way she made coffee. Impressed with the girl's natural, wacky sense of humor, he tricked her into coming on his radio show one Saturday morning. "I wanted to see if we could recreate the same nuttiness we had in the office on the air, so, just before airtime, I began kidding with her in front of the microphone, continuing the banter right into the show. It worked extremely well and she became a regular part of the program. Just to be safe, however, the writers gave her a poem in case she ever dried up (since she didn't use a script), but we never had to use it.

"Julann always followed my lead and the funny lines she said all came from her. We understood each other on the air—had a great chemistry—like George and Gracie."

One of the classic stories dealing with Julann occurred on her birthday. Dressed in an old coat, she was passing by one of New York's finer jewelry stores, when she spotted a beautiful tiara in the window. Indeed, at one time, the piece had been given by Napoleon to Josephine.

She was desperate to try it on, but the clerk informed her that this tiara was very special and could only be worn by royalty.

"*I'm* royalty," replied Julann with a poker face.

"Oh," said the clerk, not really believing her. "Who, madame, may I ask are you?"

"I'm a fairy princess," she said, "and it's my birthday."

The clerk let her try on the crown.

At the time he joined Lewis, Merv had broken off with Rita Farrell and was involved with a lady named Alice Lee Boatwright. But he was quite impressed with the comedic Miss Wright: "She had the most devastating sense of humor I'd ever come across in a woman."

Julann, on the other hand, had a much deeper reaction at their first meeting: "I felt I'd known him all my life. I believe in reincarnation and I was sure we'd been together in another existence."

Merv and Julann began to date, although not exclusively. "He'd laugh at everything I'd do," she remembers.

On their first date, Merv took Julann to see *The Most Happy Fella*, but was so tired, he fell asleep in the middle of the play.

One of the activities that both enjoyed, but not necessarily as a couple, was bowling. In fact, they regularly played with a group that included singers Julius LaRosa, Tommy Leonetti, and Lu Ann Sims; accountant Bert Adler (Julann's off-and-on steady); and Jaye P. Morgan (a regular date of Merv's).

"I was the worst player," reports Julann. "Merv *said* he was good, but he could talk us into anything."

Back at the Lewis show, the always amiable Merv was close with the entire cast and crew—except for his boss. Recalls Bob: "I was just too busy trying to be inventive and humorous every day and, as such, never really got a chance to know Merv.

"Like everyone else though, he was just marking time with my show—waiting for that big break to come along. He knew he had 'It,' but I think his lack of personal success at Warner Brothers hurt him deeply and this made him more determined than ever to want to prove himself.

"He was great in the show's sketches: was a pleasant, if not unique, singer; and the audience liked him. We did vaudeville duets together. One medley of 'Hello, My Baby' and 'Goodbye My Lady Love' was great fun.

"I know Merv did hate to wear the silly costumes for the sketches. One time, we did a bit called 'The Flying Litvaks,' a satire on tumbling acts, and we all wore leotards, which didn't set too well with him.

"Some of the shows were superb, while others were just sheer disaster."

While he was doing the stint with Lewis, Merv received an attractive offer in 1957 from ABC-TV to host their Miami-based weekend program, "Going Places." Despite the exhausting requirement that he fly to Florida each Friday night, the aspiring emcee seized this opportunity to talk for the first time on *his own show.*

"Going Places," a traveling variety program, visited a different scenic location or place of interest in southern Florida each week. One show might originate from the Miami Jai-Alai Fronton, while another would take place in Cypress Gardens, where Merv's initial program was situated.

Excited about his debut, Griffin asked his New York friends to watch the show. Unfortunately, the telecast was not the sterling success he'd hoped it would be.

"The thing started out," remembers Merv, "with George Pope, Jr., of Cypress Gardens talking about the park's water-skiing act, then he turned to me and said, 'The skiers are ready to perform, *Mirth*.'

"Later on the program, I spoke to the mayor of Miami, who called me *Herb*. The show's orchestra leader referred to me as *Mark*, and after the telecast was over, I found out that the *Miami Herald* had listed me as *Mary* Griffin, which was the lowest blow of all."

Merv's second segment of "Going Places" originated from the Gulf Stream Racetrack. It was not a show he is likely to forget either, but for reasons entirely different from the Cypress Gardens fiasco.

"About fifteen minutes before we went on the air," he recalls, "I received a phone call from my sister, Barbara. My father had just died of a heart attack. He was only fifty-five.

"I was in shock . . . completely numb, but I knew I had a live show to do and told Barbara I'd take the next plane home."

Merv went on, did the one-hour program, and didn't mention his personal tragedy until after the telecast was over. "If I'd told people, it would have affected the way they reacted to me on the air."

All of his life, Griffin has been reticent to burden others with his personal troubles, choosing, instead, to work the problems out for himself. "I guess this trait comes from my parents," he explains. "They weren't complainers either."

"Going Places" was a rather short-lived show, but it did, in part, lead to Griffin's getting an ABC evening radio program of his own near the end of 1957. Sparing no expense in this last-ditch effort to bring back live radio, the network backed the rising young star (who had quit Robert Q. Lewis) with a forty-piece orchestra and an eight-voice chorus. The daily variety show, originally running forty-five minutes in length, was increased to an hour and forty-five minutes after two months.

Scores of singers had auditioned for this show when the network announced it was looking for a host, but the shrewd, promotion-minded Merv realized that the best way to capture the prize was to approach ABC with a suggested format. To accomplish this, he enlisted the aid of Jerry Bressler and Lyn Duddy, who'd written nightclub acts for many stars. The strategy worked, because Merv got the job.

Of the program's host, the New York *Herald Tribune* would say: "Griffin is a glib, likable, emcee type."

Once the show was underway, Griffin and his staff came up with the idea of adding an attractive young girl to the cast, who could serve as a comedy foil for the star and his guest artists. The job was offered to cute, redheaded Julann Wright. She, grateful to get away from her ever-increasing secretarial duties at the Lewis program, said "Yes," pausing just momentarily to let her new employer and sometimes boyfriend do a little coaxing.

Around the end of her third week with the ABC entry, Julann paid a visit to Merv's apartment early one morning. She'd thrown a coat on over her pajamas and was somewhat upset. "They made a mistake in my check this week," she said. "I thought I ought to tell you about it right away."

"Oh, the company will adjust that," replied Griffin, inviting her in for coffee.

"But, it's a big mistake," she persisted. "They're paying me four times the salary I was hired for."

"Then, that's probably right."

"Do you mean I'm going to get that much every week?"

Merv nodded and once the realization of this newly acquired wealth sunk in, the actress excused herself. She was going out to buy something she'd always wanted—a rocking chair.

During his bachelor days, Merv had to fend for himself in the kitchen and, after awhile, became adept as a chef—at least *he* thought so. "Actually," says Julann, "he was a terrible cook, but he was thrilled and proud of everything he was able to make . . . no matter *how* it turned out.

"Once, for example, he attempted a lemon meringue pie. It wasn't even big enough to qualify as a tart.

"And, his pizzas? They were something else. English muffins covered with tomato sauce."

Although he still hadn't acquired a desire to partake in strenuous physical activities, Merv gave in to the requests of a group of friends and accompanied them one weekend to Mt. Stowe, Vermont, to try his hand at skiing.

"I should have known from the start that the experience was going to be a disaster," he confesses. "I fell off the ski lift, then, when we first started down the mountain, I twisted my ankle. I figured 'to hell with it!' It wasn't worth the work involved.

"The ski lift only went one way, so the Ski Patrol took me down the slope on a toboggan as if I had a broken leg. I was lying on the sled in front of the Red Cross hospital when a little boy came by and said, "Look, Daddy. There's a dead man!' "

For a few months, Merv had sublet Marlon Brando's New York apartment ("Marlon had a pet raccoon that left 'dirt' all over the place"), and, when he was ready to move, phoned his agent, who also represented Brando, and asked if he had another client that might be interested in taking the place.

"I was asleep one morning," he remembers, "when I was awakened by a banging at the door. (Marlon had disconnected the bell.) Groggy, and in my pajamas, I made my way to the entry and opened the door.

"Standing right in front of me was Marilyn Monroe. Our mutual agent had brought her by to see the apartment. Actually, she didn't really want it, but just had to see where the mysterious Mr. Brando lived. She stayed for a couple of hours, had fun bouncing up and down on the bed, and everyone enjoyed himself immensely."

These years (1954-58) in New York were ones of growth for Merv. He was promoting important business contacts and developing close friendships with some of the biggest stars in the entertainment business ("I introduced Eddie Fisher to Elizabeth Taylor"). Of greatest importance, he was gaining the practical expertise through shows like "Look Up and Live," "Robert Q. Lewis," "Going Places," and his own program that he would need to climb even further in his chosen profession.

Nevertheless, there were career adjustments to be made. After six years together, Merv terminated his relationship with manager Bullets Durgom. He felt that Durgom was spending too much time with his most successful client, Jackie Gleason, and, therefore, couldn't give his career the attention he felt it required. There were no hard feelings in the parting; Bullets understood Merv's position perfectly and the men remain good friends to this day.

Griffin had lost the services of the capable Mr. Durgom, but he was still in good shape as far as representation was concerned. Agent Marty Kummer of MCA had a lot of faith in this talented thirty-three-year-old, and, after months of effort, was on the verge of propelling his client into an area of entertainment Griffin had never tried before—television game shows.

Five

Americans have always been enthralled with television game shows. Despite the never-ending hail of critical bullets these programs have received over the years—including a Congressional threat to their survival during the late fifties—they have remained one of the few enduring categories of entertainment in the ever-changing world of the "boob tube."

Viewer interest in such programs can, perhaps, be explained by two basic human instincts—the need to *compete* (if only vicariously), and, of greater significance, *greed*. For television networks, however, the scheduling of game shows is, simply, a sound fiscal practice.

In a recent interview with Morton Moss, television editor of the Los Angeles *Herald-Examiner*, Merrill Heatter and Bob Quigley, who produce such shows as "Hollywood Squares" and "Gambit," explained the dollars and cents of daytime programming: "The networks get prestige and publicity from prime-time shows, but the top game shows and soap operas are where the money is. A network has to make it in daytime or it won't make it at all. The competition for game shows has never been as strong as it is today.

"The bulk of network profits is made in the daytime. The return on a prime-time show is much less, when you compare intake to cost. We don't have to worry about stars and scripts.

"It costs $50,000 to $70,000 for a network to put together a week of a game show—and $70,000 is on the expensive side. A show has thirty spots to fill for a five-day week. It's $12,000 a commercial minute of 'Hollywood Squares.' Now, multiply thirty times $12,000. That's $360,000.''

The whole idea of game shows started back in the mid-thirties when radio was king. They were then called "quiz" or "giveaway" programs. Debuting in 1936 were radio's first two major quizzes—"Uncle Jim's Question Bee," heard over the Blue network, and the better known "Professor Quiz," a CBS entry. Another show, "Spelling Bee," was scheduled on the Blue Network the following year, but it wasn't until 1938 that this sort of entertainment was being heard in any quantity over the airwaves.

One popular series was "Kay Kyser's Kollege of Musical Knowledge," which had the band-leader—referred to on the program as "The Old Professor," or "Fez"—asking contestants rather elementary questions, then giving them an obvious clue that would, almost invariably, tip the correct answer. The light, humorous NBC show featured zany "Ish Kabibble," in the person of Mervyn Bogue, as well as singer Ginny Sims and the King Sisters.

Another NBC entry to debut in 1938 was a panel show, "Information, Please!" which lasted fourteen years. Moderated by Clifton Fadiman, and featuring cynical pianist Oscar Levant as one of the panelists, the program awarded a set of the *Encyclopedia Britannica* to any listener who submitted a question the panel couldn't answer.

In 1939, there were two more NBC giveaways—"Pot O' God," on which listeners were phoned and given the opportunity to answer questions for money, and "Dr. I.Q." This quiz, sponsored by Mars, the makers of various candy bars, was unique in that it originated from a different movie theater each week. Contestants seated in the audience were asked questions. If they answered correctly, they received as many as seventy-five silver dollars. Losers got a box of Milky Way bars and two passes to the following week's movie.

The 1940s found the radio airwaves saturated with game programs. There was "Take It or Leave It," which introduced the famous $64 question; "It Pays to Be Ignorant," a satire of panel shows like "Information Please!"; "Grand Slam," patterned after Bridge; and "Quick as a Flash," featuring a murder mystery skit that contestants had to solve. Art Linkletter's "People Are Funny" and Ralph Edwards' "Truth or Consequences" (with the infamous Beulah the Buzzer) varied the question and answer formula by having contestants perform amusing stunts in exchange for prizes, while "Queen for a Day" starring Jack Bailey and "Strike It Rich" with Warren Hull awarded gifts to the lady who told the most moving sob story.

Not every audience participation program emphasized the quiz aspect of the show. Many of these entries were, simply, vehicles for a clever master-of-ceremonies to have fun with his guests. Groucho Marx was a prime example of this type of host. When his "You Bet Your Life" debuted over ABC in 1947 (and later went to television), it was obvious from the start that the questions were secondary in importance to the interview, in which this fugitive from *A Night at the Opera* poked fun at the contestants.

No guest ever left Groucho's show empty-handed. Should one of them draw a zero in the formal quiz, the host always had a consolation question that put twenty-five dollars into the contestant's pocket. That question was almost invariably the same every time: "Who's buried in Grant's tomb?"

Surprisingly, there were some who missed that one also.

Compared to the prizes of today, jackpots awarded to contestants prior to and during the Second World War were rather modest—usually not exceeding a few hundred dollars. But, after the fighting ended, the situation changed. Factories stopped manufacturing the machinery of war, and, instead, began making the luxuries of peace. Bigger and better-made automobiles, washing machines, refrigerators, and the like became available to the public in large quantities and it was the dream of most Americans to own these prestigious items.

Astute quiz program producers realized that their shows would be enhanced if large prizes were awarded to winning contestants. After all, a jackpot of tantalizing merchandise that grew in size every week would definitely sustain listener interest until some lucky person—and it could be *you*—won the whole bundle.

ABC's "Stop the Music," debuting in 1948, was one of the more popular entries in this category. Each week, host Bert Parks would phone people all over the country and ask them to identify the tune that was being sung by vocalist Kay Armen or Dick Brown, or being played by Harry Salter and his orchestra. If the party answered correctly, he received a gift, then got an opportunity to name the "Mystery Melody" for the giant jackpot of prizes, which grew every week. Sometimes it was months before a contestant won the ultimate award, but every Sunday evening families all over the United States sat glued to their radios—knowing that it could be their home that Bert Parks would be calling next.

Television had been with us since the twenties, but it wasn't until the late forties that this revolutionary new invention began to make a significant impact on the American way of life. In 1947, fourteen thousand homes in the country had televisions, and regular programs like "Kulka, Fran and Ollie," "Meet the Press," and "Kraft Television Theatre" began to be telecast. By the end of the following year, the number of sets had grown to one hundred ninety thousand.

During these early days of television, networks made it a point to schedule audience participation programming in abundance since game shows were inexpensive to produce. Three such shows, refugees from radio ("Who Said That?" with Bob Trout, "Winner Take All" featuring Bud Collyer, and "Break the Bank" starring Bert Parks), debuted on the tube in 1948. Indeed, many TV quiz formats that have aired over the years ("Dr. I.Q.," "Twenty Questions," "The Quiz Kids") were originally created for a *listening* audience.

Television panel shows—underscoring the wit and charm of the celebrity players, rather than the mechanics of the game itself—have been in vogue since 1950 when producers Mark Goodson and Bill Todman launched their long-running "What's My Line?" on CBS. Each week, for nearly seventeen years, the panel, comprised of regulars Dorothy Kilgallen, Arlene Francis, and Bennett Cerf, was joined by a guest member, such as Steve Allen, whose question "Is it bigger than a bread box?" has become legend, and together they attempted to determine the occupations of "civilian" contestants, as well as the identity of a famous mystery guest. Former newscaster John Daly hosted the program, which, after its demise on the network, began anew in the syndicated market.

Two other early panel offerings from the Goodson-Todman organization were "I've Got a Secret," debuting in 1952, with Garry Moore and a group of regulars that included Bill Cullen, Jayne Meadows, Henry Morgan, and Betsy Palmer; and "To Tell The Truth," making its initial appearance in 1957, and moderated by Bud Collyer. The panel on this show changed regularly, but Tom Poston, Kitty Carlisle, and Orson Bean seemed to be more permanent than most.

Patterning itself after the ever successful "You Bet Your Life" with Groucho Marx was another popular quiz program that debuted in 1953. On "Two for the Money," comedian Herb Shriner traded banter with contestants, while Dr. Mason Gross of Rutgers University refereed the question and answer part of the show.

There were other games on the air in the early fifties. "Beat the Clock," "The Name's the Same," "Songs for Sale,""Masquerade Party," "Name that Tune," and "Dollar a Second" were among the viewers' favorites. But, in 1955, networks and program producers decided that a new element was needed to instill fresh life into the overdone giveaway show format. What they came up with was the big-money quiz.

The first of these programs to debut was "The $64,000 Question," hosted by Hal March. Contestants who professed extraordinary knowledge on a particular subject were isolated on stage in a sound-proof booth—to prevent their hearing remarks from the audience—and asked questions so involved and detailed that even professional experts might miss them. If the multi-parted query was answered correctly, the player doubled the amount of money he'd won the previous week. The maximum prize was, of course, $64,000. If wrong, he or she lost everything and was awarded a new Cadillac as a consolation prize.

One well-remembered contender, with whom Mr. and Mrs. America sweated along as he struggled to answer the questions March asked, was New York shoemaker Gino Prato. A self-styled expert in Grand Opera, Mr. Prato garnered $32,000 before he decided to take his winnings and depart.

Other players on the show were Dr. Joyce Brothers, fielding queries about prize fighting, and actress Barbara Feldon, later of "Get Smart" fame, whose topic was Shakespeare.

"The $100,000 Big Surprise" came next, hosted initially by Jack Barry, then Mike Wallace; and was followed by "The $64,000 Challenge." This entry matched the top money winners of "The $64,000 Question" against each other. One confrontation was between actor Vincent Price and jockey Billy Pearson—both authorities on art. Sonny Fox was the first host of the show, but he was replaced by Ralph Story.

Finally, there was perhaps the most exciting of all the big money quizzes—"Twenty-One." Players on this show, who competed against each other, had to be "walking encyclopedias," since host Jack Barry asked them difficult questions about a variety of topics. On the plus side, however, the format was structured so that, as long as he kept beating his opponent, a lucky contestant could win an unlimited amount of momey.

Neilsen ratings on these shows soared to the top of the charts, especially on weeks that a continuing champion was trying to increase his bankroll. The program-makers had correctly predicted that the public would identify with the more successful contestants—perspiring at home along with them as the super brains reached to the depths of their memory banks for the answers to the impossible questions they were asked.

Few who watched Charles Van Doren's sweat-beaded brow as he built his winnings to well over one hundred thousand dollars can forget those tense moments. During his tenure on "Twenty-One," the slender college professor was elevated to celebrity status. His picture appeared on the cover of major magazines and there were even offers to star in movies.* Much of America was truly saddened on the night he was ultimately defeated by a lady lawyer—Vivienne Nearing. It was as if a national folk hero had died.

For the better part of three years, the mammoth quiz shows fascinated television audiences. The bubble had to give way sometime, and when it did, it didn't burst—it *exploded!*

In the autumn of 1958, Mr. Edward Higemeir, who had been a standby player on a program called "Dotto," claimed that winners on that series had been given answers to questions in advance of the show by the producer. The executive supposedly had paid Higemeir and a losing contestant a total of $5,500 in return for their silence.

Herbert Stempel, who'd lost his championship on "Twenty-One" to Charles Van Doren, was the next ex-contender to speak out. He alleged that he'd been coached by the producers of the program on how to react in the isolation booth and had even been given advance information as to what he'd be asked. When Van Doren came on the show, Stempel was instructed to throw the match and, although he'd left the series many thousands of dollars richer, his conscience had dictated that he come forward and expose the truth.

Weeks went by and more disgruntled contestants stepped forward to tell how the particular show they'd appeared on had been rigged. The public began shouting "Fraud!" and "Fake!" Ratings on the questionable quizzes nosedived, and soon our representatives in Washington, D.C., took a more than passing interest in what all the commotion was about. There was no law against this sort of devious programming, but some politicians felt that there *should* be one.

Networks and producers vehemently denied that

anything irregular had taken place on the "tainted" programs, yet, after extensive investigation by a district attorney, grand jury, and Congressional committee, the truth was finally learned. Television executives admitted that quiz shows were "controlled" to a certain extent so that they could be made more entertaining to home viewers. The on-camera dramatics in both the reading and answering of questions, the choice of contestants with high audience appeal, and the feeding of answers to players to manipulate suspense were, according to these men, necessary if the programs were to sustain their superiority in the ratings race.

The legislators disagreed with the producers' contentions that, since nobody was really hurt, their clandestine maneuvers to provide entertainment should be sanctioned. The *people* had been hoodwinked and this could not be tolerated. Not only were new laws passed to forbid similar transgressions in the future, but several witnesses who had lied during the grand jury investigation pleaded guilty to charges of perjury.

Shows were dropped, jobs lost, careers destroyed, and reputations tarnished. CBS-TV invoked a ban on giveaway programs which lasted fourteen years.

Over at NBC and ABC, big money prizes were eliminated from those shows that had survived the purge and these series were, in turn, subjected to careful surveillance by professional investigators hired by the networks.

The credibility of television game shows had received one hell of a "shiner" and it was, indeed, questionable whether a total recovery was possible.

ABC's six-million-dollar attempt to resurrect live radio was a flop, a *big* flop, and, as a result, Merv's entertaining show was cancelled. (The program had supposedly been raking in eighteen thousand fan letters per week.) Rather than sit around and feel sorry for himself ("I've been cancelled so many times, they use me as a tax write-off"), the performer decided to take an extended vacation in the Caribbean.

A few sunny weeks later, he received an urgent wire from Marty Kummer, his agent at MCA, asking him to rush home. Goodson/Todman Productions, the successful game show factory, were seeking a host for a new CBS entry they'd created, entitled "Play Your Hunch."

"The format was similar to 'To Tell the Truth,' " recalls Mark Goodson, "in that the contestant had to guess which guest was real and which were the phonies. Missing was the cross-examination that 'Truth' employed."

Merv read over the "script" for the pilot show, yet, in truth, was not too excited about the prospect of doing a game program. Nevertheless, trusting Kummer's judgment, he agreed to be at the audition at seven that evening.

Griffin: "I arrived at the appointed place at seven sharp and a secretary came out and asked me to wait. After about fifteen minutes of warming the bench, I decided, 'To hell with it!' I was standing by the elevator, when the woman came out again, asked where I was going, and then said, 'They're ready for you.'

"As I went in, I heard somebody announce, 'and here's the star of our show . . . Merv Griffin!'

"What I found was a room full of Goodson/Todman staff members, pretending to be a studio audience. 'Oh!' I said, a bit surprised, 'we're playing for keeps?'

"And that's just what I did. I'd studied the show format, so I knew what was expected. I did interviews with the audience, played the game, and, after we were done, Goodman called me into his office and confessed he couldn't believe I'd never done a game show before. I was hired on the spot."

According to Goodson, Griffin was chosen because while he was interviewing the contestants, he *listened* to what they were saying. Merv: "This is no effort for me. I'm not even conscious of it. Maybe I'm just curious, but I like to ask people questions about themselves."

Since "Play Your Hunch" didn't deal in huge money prizes, it really wasn't affected by the quiz show scandals (except that monitors were present to insure security), which were hogging the daily headlines in 1958. Making its daytime debut mid-year, the program received good notices from critics (the *New York Post* called it "the best of the new arrivals") with particular note taken of the fact that affable Griffin was emphasizing entertainment, rather than mere questions and answers, and also conducted some very enjoyable interviews.

Everything Merv had ever learned since he entered show business came into play when he began doing "Hunch": "It was the type of show that gave a performer the chance to use his complete bag of tricks. I sang . . . led the orchestra . . . danced . . . acted in sketches—all as part of the stunts to test the panel.

"As with any impromptu show, there were a number of uncomfortable moments. We had three girls on as Wave lieutenants, and the contestants had to guess which one was authentic.

"One contestant said, 'It can't be "Miss X" because her shoes aren't shined; her skirt isn't pressed. Not only that, but she doesn't speak with any authority.'

"Naturally, she was the real Wave. What could I do? I apologized to her on the air, but the armed services were furious and refused to cooperate with us from that point."

"Play Your Hunch" was rather unique. Within its

lifetime, it aired on all three networks. After CBS cancelled the program, it was picked up by ABC, and, later, after eight months off the air, found another home at NBC. At one point, it even had a prime-time version.

When the show went to NBC, Merv, for the first time, got involved with its production aspects. "I had some new ideas that I wanted incorporated into the format," he explains.

Griffin enjoyed the show, since it gave him the opportunity to polish his emcee skills. "You can have more fun with ordinary people in half an hour than you can, maybe in a whole year with people who have to work at trying to be funny. And that's the sort of people I dealt with on that show. You'd come up with real, honest-to-goodness humor on daytime television, whereas nighttime TV, especially in the late fifties, was much more formal. The situation I ran up against every day was almost like improvising in an acting class. You couldn't help but have fun."

While he was doing "Hunch," Merv came up with the idea of forming his own orchestra. During his time off, he wanted to take it on the road to play in nightclubs and concerts. The group was to introduce a new sound called "Razzmajazz." As Merv described the theory: "First we play an old song as it was originally written and recorded. Then we do a second chorus as it might be played today, then combine the two styles in the third chorus. For example, if we were to do a Count Basie number, the third chorus might be a combination of Basie and cha-cha-cha."

Merv Griffin and his "Play Your Hunch" band, for one reason or another, never really progressed beyond the idea stage; but the star still retains his lifelong dream to, someday, lead a symphony orchestra.

When he was first signed by Goodson/Todman,

Merv—still the happy bachelor—resided in an apartment on a dead-end street in Manhattan's East Fifties, which overlooked the East River and the United Nations Building. "I let the various girls I was dating decorate the place," explains Merv, "and that's why the colors and ideas in the furniture didn't really match."

He lived alone, except for a red mongrel dog named Poochie. Merv: "I got her free from an adoption home for dogs, but I paid fifty dollars a month extra rent because Poochie had to have a terrace. I had to sit in baggage cars on trains, and walk out in the snow and wind on winter nights—all for Poochie."

The summer of 1958 found Merv, with friends Bob Barry (an agent), Rose Tobias (an assistant to producer David Susskind), and a struggling musician named Burt Bacharach, renting a house at Ocean Beach on Fire Island. ("The theatrical and writing crowds spent their summers there.")

Bacharach obtained a job in a small bar on the island, playing piano to very few customers. One weekend, a reviewer from *Variety* just happened to be there and, as a gag, wrote a glowing review of the songwriter-pianist. "The following weekend," recalls Merv, "the place was packed—mostly with drunks, who got angry at Burt because he refused to play their requests. I had to run interference to see that he didn't get punched."

On another weekend, a program director at CBS decided to throw a party for his show biz friends, and, for entertainment, hired a Flamenco group. Merv, who had been enjoying his host's liquid refreshment, thought he'd try his hand at this Spanish dance, but, just to make it challenging, decided to do his thing on the roof: "When I fell, I missed a boulder by three inches and landed in a patch of poison ivy. They carried me off the island in an ambulance. I never went back.

"I wound up with a back injury and, whenever I'm

under pressure, the thing still bothers me."

With "Play Your Hunch" cancelled by both CBS and ABC, and his only current job being on NBC radio's "It's Network Time" (a talk show), Merv nevertheless married Julann Wright early in 1959.

Merv: "Julann and I had dated off and on for several years. Suddenly I just realized that I was crazy about her and that she was the only one I enjoyed being with."

Julann: "We had a friendship that grew into love. I wasn't too surprised when he asked me to marry him, but playing the woman's game, I pretended I was.

"We had always acted like a couple of kids together and, one day, we were driving along when he started laughing so hard at a joke, Merv had to pull over to the side of the road until he could compose himself.

"While we were sitting there, I told him I had discovered a gray hair. He said he had one, too, and added, 'Let's get married and we'll have two gray hairs.' That started us laughing all over again. We went into a restaurant, still giggling, and, all of a sudden, I realized I had been proposed to."

Two months later, the couple eloped, flying to Norfolk, Virginia, where they were married by a friend of Merv's—a Navy chaplain. The simple ceremony was witnessed by a Navy lieutenant and his wife.

"While we were waiting for our Wasserman tests in Norfolk," Merv recalls, "I picked up a local paper and read Walter Winchell's column. He had a real scoop. According to him, Jaye P. Morgan and I were about to tie the knot and were seen together shopping for furniture."

The realization that he was married first came to Merv three days after the wedding when his new bride began moving her things into his bachelor apartment: "She brought furniture, her paints, her materials for ceramics, and her carpentry tools. Imagine marrying a girl and having her bring her trousseau and discovering a saw, a hammer, and a drill! I was afraid to go to sleep that night."

Julann: "My father had four daughters. Someone had to learn to use tools to help him."

The bride found that the most important adjustment *she* had to make when she moved into Merv's quarters was to Poochie. "She had always been fond of me," Julann explains, "but that first week, when I got all of the attention, she just sat in front of Merv's chair and glared at me. Modern science came to my rescue, however. I won her over with dog candy."

Mrs. Merv Griffin, Jr., immediately hit it off with Mrs. Merv Griffin, Sr., and, in fact, they began a small business together. Rita, unable to find suitable decorative pictures for her grandchildren's rooms (daughter Barbara had married a pharmacist named William Eyre), made some three-dimensional ones. Some stores, quite taken with the unusual artistic creations, suggested she manufacture them. She did just that, working on the West Coast, while her new daughter-in-law was doing the same thing in the east. The business, known as "Rita's Rogues," grew eventually to include the manufacture of puffed cloth dolls, sold in department stores and through mail-order houses. By 1960, Merv had invested in the company, which was employing fourteen women, and projecting a total sale that year of ten thousand units at $9.95 each.

Aside from rejoining Robert Q. Lewis after Merv's ABC radio program went off the air, Julann had been a part-time Avon lady when she'd married, but quit the route shortly thereafter. Says Griffin: "She really didn't have much luck as a saleslady. Her territory was the tenements and nobody there could afford the products. Also, Julann would feel so sorry for these people that, if they were ill, she'd take them to the hospital, which took up a lot of her time."

The first year they were together, Julann told her husband about a black woman she'd met up in Harlem, who was trying to help black children learn things they weren't absorbing in their regular schooling. Impressed with what this teacher was accomplishing, the entertainer bought her the tables and chairs necessary for a more formal classroom.

Merv's professional activities in 1959-61 were quite varied.

He wrote and recorded two songs, "Eternally" with Hugo Winterhalter and his orchestra, and "Hot-Cha-Cha" with Mitch Miller. These tunes didn't succeed too well, but two later recordings, "Banned in Boston," and "Charanga" hit the top twenty on the charts.

Before "Hunch" was finally picked up by NBC, Griffin acted as moderator (replacing Carl Reiner) on ABC-TV's ad-lib marathon. "Keep Talking" ("the first time I got big money—*$1,500 per show*—for my television work"); made regular appearances on "The Arthur Murray Party," a song-and-dance spectacular; substituted for vacationing host Bud Collyer on "To Tell the Truth"; and was one of several singing stars on a replacement series, "Music for a Summer Night."

Griffin also hosted "Saturday Prom," NBC's unfortunate 1960 attempt to cash in on the success of Dick Clark's "American Bandstand" show at ABC. "Unlike Clark's program," says Merv, "we had a live orchestra, led by Bobby Vinton, and five hundred kids dancing to his music."

"I asked a friend what he thought of the first show. He said that it 'looked like an auto accident.' "

Late in 1961, Griffin did an entry of the "DuPont Show of the Week" series, *The Wonderful World of Toys*. "Harpo Marx was in that one," according to Merv. "We were in Central Park and I was just about to sing a number when a pigeon came along and crapped on my head.

" 'Wonderful!' shouted Harpo. 'That's good luck! That means the show will be a hit.' "

Anthony Patrick Griffin, Merv and Julann's only child, was born on December 8, 1959—the same day that "Play Your Hunch" debuted on NBC. Naturally, the proud father made an on-the-air announcement of the arrival of his heir.

A few months after Tony's birth, the Griffins bought a twenty-acre farm in Califon, New Jersey. They still maintained their New York apartment, but the couple also wanted a place where they could breathe fresh air. As Julann, who had retired from show business, explained it: "The wonderful thing about being in the country is that you feel you are in a special world all your own. One of the troubles with New York is that, once you get out of your apartment, there's no place to sit down unless you go into a restaurant for a cup of coffee or a hamburger. Out here, the whole world is yours."

Poochie also enjoyed her new environment. Merv: "She bayed at the moon and went crazy when you brought a chicken into the house. Not only that, she looked so much like a fox, we considered putting lights and diamond bracelets on her paws so nobody would take a shot at her."

The early American farm, known as Teetertown, consisted of the main house, a guest house, a stable (so that Merv could eventually rear quarterhorses), a historic mill, barn, a bathhouse, two waterfalls, three ponds, and a swimming pool. It also had an infamous past.

"A book was written about the place," reports Merv. "About one hundred sixty years before we moved in, there'd been a murder in the house. This minister had

141

killed his wife with apples injected with arsenic. He was the last man publicly hanged in the state of New Jersey."

Julann Wright Griffin is a very bright lady, but she is also a self-admitted kook, and this aspect of her delightful personality certainly flourished in the wilds of New Jersey. Indeed, with her interests in Chinese tomatoes and grasshopper pie, Merv lovingly began to refer to her as "my abstract wife."

He recalls: "Someone told her that we had weeds on our property which were very decorative if you sprayed them white. So, she sprayed them on the lawn. When I came home, a whole patch of lawn was white. I was furious. The next day, I came home and the lawn, wasn't white anymore. She'd sprayed it green. Naturally, the wrong color green."

There was also an invasion of ladybugs, courtesy of Julann. Says Merv: "She became concerned about reports that chemical sprays caused cancer, so she decided to grow her own vegetables. What she didn't figure on were the aphids.

"Well, she read a few books, learned that ladybugs eat aphids, and ordered two thousand of them. The box said 'keep refrigerated.' She forgot to tell me that and I went to the fridge for a midnight snack and, there were twelve thousand legs waving at me.

"The instructions were to use one tablespoonful of ladybugs every day. The next morning, I heard blood-curdling screams from the garden. There stood Julann holding an empty spoon. She was covered with ladybugs from top to bottom."

Of course, Merv couldn't really brag about his agricultural skills either, as Julann reports: "He was a terrible farmer, but a great organizer. He was the chief among us Indians. In other words, he'd hold the ladder while I hung the curtains.

"He loved riding around on the tractor, but he hated mowing the lawn. Actually, we had a caretaker who really worked the farm.

"Merv had put on some weight when we first bought the place, and, one day when he went out to the stable, a colt bit him in his flabby middle. He maintained a distance from the animals for awhile after that."

After awhile, "Play Your Hunch" became a very undemanding assignment for Merv. Though it certainly provided him a comfortable living and let him talk ("I was speaking my own words—using my *brain*"), from a practical standpoint he was nowhere near to achieving the household name status every entertainer longs for.

(It's unfortunate, but game show hosts are seemingly always in plentiful supply and, in daytime television, a performer can only garner a personal following from a limited segment of the population.)

With his vast creative energy, what Merv really needed was a break that would allow him to make use of his full talents in a *prime-time* situation and thereby lead the way to major stardom. That break came, strictly by accident, in the form of late night talk show host, Jack Paar.

"I was doing my live show one afternoon," muses Griffin, "when, all of a sudden, there was a gasp from the studio audience and then big applause. I looked around and there was Paar walking out from behind the curtains. He looked at me, and I looked at him, both of us equally shocked. I said, 'What do you want?' and he replied, 'What are you doing here?'

"What had happened was incredible," continues Merv. "Paar had always used that particular studio as a shortcut to his own offices. Unbeknown to him, we were moved into it that day while our regular studio was being renovated. So Jack walked through, as usual, totally unaware he was walking into a confrontation with me and my audience."

There was no way Merv could have known then what a profound effect this chance encounter was about to have on his career.

Six

In the fickle macrocosm known as television, few things remain constant. A clever personality catches the attention of viewers and, for a time, becomes a hot show business property. Yet, once the public has tired of him, he may quickly slip back into oblivion.

Programming trends also change regularly. One season there might be two dozen westerns or situation comedies on the tube, but, a year or so later, these entries may have been replaced by a block of police or detective shows.

Conversely, there are a minority of program categories which always seem to be well represented on the airwaves—public affairs, audience participation, soap operas, and, of course, the entertainment talk show. Although the quality of these chatter programs has diminished in recent years, the genre is, at this writing, ably embodied by such stalwarts as Johnny Carson, Mike Douglas, Dinah Shore, and, of course, Merv.

It is the type of show that is never likely to disappear from the television screen completely, since, aside from the generous salary usually paid the host or hostess, these programs are relatively inexpensive to produce and bring in a good financial return for stations that broadcast them.

During the often unimaginative infant days of network programming, the concept of a late night show primarily devoted to variety and conversation was rather revolutionary. Indeed, cries of "Impossible!" and "It'll never work!" were heard all over Madison Avenue.

The man who conceived this wild idea was Mr. Sylvester L. "Pat" Weaver, Vice-President, and later Chairman of the Board, of the National Broadcasting Company. Weaver, described by many of his peers as a programming genius, once wrote: "Television is the educator and the communicator, the informer, the thing that can inspire and enrich man as he makes his greatest transition from what he is today into the first genuine adult human being."

While he was at the network, Weaver attempted to make this theory a reality. The executive is credited with originating the concepts for and scheduling such well-known programs as "Your Show of Shows" with Sid Caesar and Imogene Coca; "Howdy Doody"; "Ding Dong School"; "The All Star Revue," "Colgate Comedy Hour"; "Zoo Parade"; and "Wide, Wide World." He wanted to make television its "own medium," rather than "radio with pictures." To help accomplish this metamorphosis, he developed the practice of network originated and produced shows, a departure from the common method of depending on advertising agencies for programming material.

Attempting to entice after-hours viewers away from the ancient movies being shown by local television stations, Pat set "Broadway Open House," a live variety show, for nightly airing at eleven o'clock (EST). Hopefully, the ready-made program would attract affiliate stations, who would abandon their films in favor of this fresh new concept.

The lighthearted entry, debuting in May of 1950, was originally supposed to have a comic named Don "Creesh" Hornsby as its star, but the entertainer succumbed to polio two weeks before the program's premiere and, after a frantic search, Jerry Lester—dubbed "the Heckler of Hecklers"—was set as the replacement. Relieving Lester for two nights a week was the quick and witty Morey Amsterdam.

"Broadway Open House" had no set format (a first for television) and Lester's philosophy was to let each night take care of itself. The complement of regular performers included announcer Wayne Howell, singers Andy Roberts and Jane Harvey, accordionist Milton DeLugg, and the one and only Dagmar, a tall, well-endowed strawberry blond, who gave deadpan poetry readings and served as a perfect foil for the host.

The program, with its extensive use of proven vaudeville and burlesque routines, was often quite a zany experience. However, it wasn't to last. Although in some cities, the show was garnering higher viewer ratings than many prime-time presentations, the local station managers weren't overjoyed. From an economic standpoint, it was much cheaper to run an old movie for the twentieth time, rather than pay NBC for this more expensive offering that would cut into existing revenues from local sponsors. After fifteen months on the air, "Broadway Open House" closed.

In the late forties and early fifties, network programming didn't start until two in the afternoon, since executives felt it would be difficult to draw an audience at an earlier hour. Weaver, maverick that he was, disagreed with this thinking and conceived a program designed to wake people up and inform them what had happened in the world while they were asleep. Inexpensive to produce, the "Today" show was the forerunner in both mood and attitude to our present day television talk programs. It introduced the idea of the "magazine" format show (a production financed by a variety of sponsors, rather than a single backer, as had been the common practice up to then).

The morning entry debuted over the twenty-six stations in the NBC network at seven in the morning on January 14, 1952. Although the show broadcast for three hours (because of the time difference between New York and Chicago), only two hours were viewed in any particular city.

Unfortunately, that first show contained only one paid commercial, which was one more than was on some of the later telecasts in the program's initial weeks of life. After eight months on the air, "Today" was a $1.5 million flop and Weaver's critics were demanding it be cancelled.

But, the innovater believed in this program concept and resisted the cries to abandon it. Numerous attractions—beauty queens, authors, fashion shows, politicians—were tried in an attempt to lure viewers, who slowly began to make this entry a morning habit. By 1954, it was being watched by two and a half million people in forty-nine cities, and had a then-record gross annual income of eleven million dollars.

Host of the "Today" show was the delightful, easygoing Dave Garroway, who enjoyed using technical crews, camera, and equipment as props. His previously aired "Garroway at Large" variety program had been terminated in 1951 after a three year run. Described by both critics and the NBC publicity staff as possessing a "warm intimate style," the tall, bespectacled performer, a fugitive from the Chicago school of broadcasting, offered his audience a conglomeration of news, time-and-weather checks, interviews, guest performances, conversation, and his own exquisitely exotic musings.

Regulars on the program included veteran announcer Jack Lescoulie, newsman Frank Blair, and a piano-player chimpanzee, J. Fred Muggs. Old J. Fred was quite the card on camera. He worked well with

Garroway, providing many amusing impromptu moments.

Behind the scenes, however, this miniature King Kong did not endear himself to his co-workers. Aside from the fact that he was not housebroken (he seemed to enjoy urinating on furniture, crew members, guests, and, of course, Garroway), J. Fred had a habit of biting people. More than once, amiable Dave forced a smile while he concealed his injured hand from the camera.

On one occasion, the miserable monkey pulled a diamond ring from the finger of former Miss America Lee Merriwether, and it took several crew members to get him to release the valuable from his mouth. Continued incidents like this eventually led to Mr. Muggs' early retirement.

The ground floor studio from which "Today" was telecast had large show windows that presented a candid view of New York's 49th Street. Each day, innumerable faces pressed against the glass to watch the show that was going on inside and, often, these specators wound up on national television. One morning found the countenance of President Harry S. Truman unexpectedly at the window, peering about to see what in the world everyone was gawking at. The Chief Executive had been taking his morning constitutional, accompanied by an army of Secret Service agents and entertainer George Jessel. Though invited by a production aide to come inside and join Garroway on the program, the President politely refused.

Placards were often seen at the window. Nearly every morning, viewers were exposed to large signs bearing messages akin to "Ban the Bomb," "Jesus Saves," "Sale at Macy's," "Susie Come Home—We Love You," and "Burma Shave." One bold television personality, whose program aired on another network *opposite* "Today," had his aides flash a sign suggesting that viewers switch their dials to his show.

Garroway stayed with "Today" until 1961, when he was replaced by John Chancellor, who relinquished that spot two years later to Hugh Downs.

It's said that imitation is the most sincere form of flattery. 1954 found CBS trying to grab some of the early morning advertising revenues with a two hour entry, patterned after its NBC competition, entitled "The Morning Show." Among that doomed program's various hosts were newsman Walter Cronkite, who was supported by the Bil and Cora Baird puppets, Jack Paar, and, as previously mentioned, Merv, substituting for Dick Van Dyke.

The "Today" show was finally a hit, and Pat Weaver decided to launch another of his ideas. In 1954, he scheduled "Home," described as a daily "service magazine of the air," aimed at women. With lovely Arlene Francis as its hostess, the innovative program stayed on the tube nearly four years.

Although "Broadway Open House" had been a failure, Weaver was convinced that the late evening hours could prove to be profitable for the network. When it was suggested to him that he have Steve Allen, complete with horn-rimmed glasses, take over the time slot once occupied by Lester and Amsterdam, he was quite interested in the idea. Allen was then hosting a late night show on WNBT, the NBC owned-and-operated station in New York.

According to Weaver, the problem with "Open House" was that the basic format—a frantic burlesque show—was completely wrong for such a late hour. What was needed was a program akin to the "Today" show—warm, relaxed, with a stronger emphasis on entertainment. After studying the versatile Mr. Allen on the local New York station, the executive knew that this was the man who could provide that sort of production.

150

The "Tonight" show starring Steve Allen had debuted on WNBT, from eleven to midnight, on July 23, 1953. Gene Rayburn served as announcer and the orchestra was conducted by Bobby Bryne. House singer was young Steve Lawrence, who was joined a few weeks later by another newcomer, Eydie Gorme.

If nothing else, Allen's program was certainly spontaneous. Even he didn't know what he was going to do from night to night. He might decide to play the piano in his pajamas, have a barber cut his hair, or a dentist work on his teeth. Nothing was too far out for Steve.

As a disc jockey on KNX (the CBS affiliate in Los Angeles) from 1948 to 1950, Allen had become one of Southern California's most popular and unique radio personalities. Listeners to his program for nightowls, which was presented before a small studio audience, could count on hearing jazz records; some off-hand remarks on music; interviews with movie or nightclub stars who dropped by to plug their newest film, record, or appearance; and the wonderful crazy ad-libs of the host who seldom read a commercial as written.

There was an evening when his scheduled guest did not appear and Steve, desperate to fill the rest of the show, walked out into the house, carrying a heavy floor mike, and began trading quips with the audience. Utilizing his quick wit, the host turned the experience into a hilarious one, later making these audience interviews a regular part of his program. All of the basic elements that make up today's television talk programs were present in Allen's KNX radio show.

Moving to New York in 1950, Steve did a variety of shows for CBS-TV—"Songs for Sale," "The Steve Allen Show," and "What's My Line?" When that network decided to concentrate on the career of a new comedian named Jackie Gleason instead of his, the

151

entertainer (who, incidentally, is a prolific song writer—"This Could Be the Start of Something Big") accepted the offer at WNBT.

When Allen's local show moved to the network, its cast remained virtually intact, although two new singers now shared the spotlight with Steve and Eydie. The girl's name was Pat Marshall and she was joined by an unknown male vocalist, Andy Williams. Orchestra leader was Skitch Henderson.

The one-hour-forty-five-minute (it would later lose fifteen minutes) "Tonight" show debuted on September 27, 1954. It was not broadcast from a television studio as had been the case when it was done exclusively for WNBT, but from the eight-hundred-seat Hudson Theater, a former Broadway legit house.

Like its predecessor, "Broadway Open House," "Tonight" had problems in gaining acceptance from the NBC affiliates around the country. These local stations were content to run their old movies or other inexpensive programs, rather than pay for this more costly late night entry. Ergo, the show's initial audience was limited to the viewing areas of the five NBC owned-and-operated stations.

Allen drew ingredients from both "Today" and "Broadway Open House," mixed in many elements he'd first employed on his KNX radio program, then spiced the concoction with a new gimmick or two, and came up with a highly entertaining show with a set format that often gave way to the unexpected. Sight gags, remote telecasts from places and events of interest, audience interviews, and just about any other device that would prove interesting or fun to viewers were employed by this genius showman. Indeed, many features first introduced by Allen on this comparatively low budget show have become standard components of today's comedy-variety programs in prime-time.

From the beginning, Allen was able to draw top celebrities (Fred MacMurray, Judy Garland, Elizabeth Taylor, Van Johnson) to his program to either entertain or simply talk. Unknown performers like Don Adams were given an opportunity to showcase their talents; authors came on to plug their new books; concerned experts on one subject or another discussed serious matters; and, finally, there were the screwball guests. These included everyone from a man who planned to parachute from the top of the Empire State Building to another who put his hand into an aquarium full of man-eating piranha fish. No matter who the guests were, they all received the same fee—AFTRA scale of $240.

Allen thrived on his audience sessions, making them an integral part of the show. As a reward for chatting with the host, cooperative civilians often received Allen's favorite prize—a large salami. Not wanting to exclude the people in the balcony from participation, on occasion Steve would climb a tall ladder—microphone in hand—in order to interview them also.

He loved pulling wild stunts and often did so as an opening teaser for the program. As viewers tuned in the telecast each night, they might find the star selling hot dogs on the street outside the theater or dressed as Superman, asking a passerby for directions. One such opening, executed while the show was visiting Miami Beach, had a unit of U.S. Marines invading the shoreline—a stunt which put the uninformed guests at the city's plush hotels into a minor panic.

Besides being a master at satire (his partially-scripted/ partially ad-lib skits were a popular feature on the show), Steve also had his serious side. There were single guest programs (Carl Sandburg); and single topic shows (narcotics, Negro music, the Bomb); and evenings when he spouted off on a particular cause, such as the need to rid America's labor unions of racketeers. That particular program resulted in telephone threats against the host, the tires of his automobile being slashed, and a stink bomb being set off in the theater.

With the show garnering high ratings, affiliate stations began to schedule it. One-minute commercial spots, which had originally sold to sponsors for $4500, increased to $6700—and the program was costing a mere $42,000 per week to produce.

In 1956, Allen was one of the brightest stars in television and NBC decided to give him a prime-time variety show on Sunday nights—designed to steal some viewers from CBS's Ed Sullivan. These new duties were to be performed in addition to his "Tonight" assignment, although to relieve a portion of his work load, the network agreed to install a substitute host on the eleven-thirty program two evenings per week. That host turned out to be the cigar-smoking comedian, Ernie Kovaks.

Pressures from the Sunday night program ultimately led to Steve's having to abandon the "Tonight" show altogether. His final appearance as host, at which time he recalled the highlights of his years on the program, aired on January 25, 1957.

Years later, Allen would try a more subdued talk show format in the syndicated market, but would not achieve success akin to what he enjoyed on "Tonight."

NBC wasn't too sure what to do after Allen left the late night show. Almost in desperation, they changed the title to "Tonight: America After Dark" and set announcer Jack Lescoulie as anchor man of a team of noted newspaper columnists. They included Hy Gardner, Earl Wilson, Vernon Scott, Irv Kupcinet, Bob Considine, and Paul Coates. The members of the fourth estate would report—via mobile units—on what the country did during its evenings.

This cross between "Today" and the network news

was a bomb. Advertising revenues disappeared almost as fast as the loyal audience Allen had built for that hour. Soon, Lescoulie was replaced by disc jockey Al "Jazzbo" Collins, but he didn't last long either. Collins departed the show on July 26, 1957.

Totally revamped, "Tonight" was back on the air three nights later, but now it had a new host. His name was Jack "I kid you not" Paar.

This native of Canton, Ohio, had previously starred in four network daytime programs (including "The Morning Show")—all of them unsuccessful. Nevertheless, Paar had achieved a reputation as being a deft entertainer who could quite quickly step into a show and make things work after having pinch-hit for Ed Sullivan and Arthur Godfrey when they were ill.

Desperate to entice Allen's sponsors and audience back to the show, the network executives (Pat Weaver had resigned in 1956) decided to take a chance on this emotional, outspoken performer. With NBC's blessings, Paar chose to turn "Tonight" into, basically, an impromptu talk show. There would be no scenery, a permanent orchestra, some audience interviews, and a few celebrity and odd-ball guests, who would, simply, wing it.

Certainly this format was the *absolute* prototype for practically all similar programs (including Merv Griffin's) that came later.

Jack Paar was anything but an overnight sensation. His show, in fact, floundered around for several months amid unfavorable reviews and low ratings. Assisted by announcer Hugh Downs, he traded amusing remarks with semi-regular guests like nutty blond Dody Goodman and hostess Elsa Maxwell, as well as a variety of other celebrities who happened to be in New York and available.

During his confrontations with the audience, he once

155

ignored Cary Grant, who'd been planted in the house as a gag, and, instead, interviewed the person sitting next to the actor. On another occasion, he decided to pick on Miss Miller, an audience regular for Steve Allen, who was now visiting Paar each night, and would later become a permanent fixture on Merv's show. "Why do you come here?" he asked the elderly lady, assuming it was for the prizes she was frequently awarded.

"Because I'm lonely," was the reply.

Feeling a bit sheepish, Paar called for a commercial.

It was October before Jack Paar started making any sort of major impact on the public. About the tenth of that month, he became involved in a rather embarrassing incident which, *fortunately*, made the newspapers.

He'd introduced a new singer on the program—a pretty teenager named Trish Dwelly, who was believed to be a non-professional. The girl was an instant hit, receiving offers for record contracts, screen tests, and a commitment to appear regularly on the "Tonight" show.

It was a fraud. A few days later, news leaked out that Miss Dwelly was no amateur. She'd sung professionally with a group, which had guested on a number of national television programs.

Mortified, Paar apologized on the air for the flim-flam, explaining that he had been too naïve to question the songstress closely about her background.

This was not the last time in his five-year reign on "Tonight" that Jack would publicly express his remorse for errors he had made. Future predicaments and open feuds with prominent persons were the factors that made "The Jack Paar Show" (as it was later called) the program people wanted to see. Over the years, for one seemingly inconsequential reason or another, the host took on Walter Winchell, Dorothy Kiigallen, Jack

O'Brian, Jimmy Hoffa, Ed Sullivan, Fred Allen, Mickey Rooney (whom he "threw" off his show), several publications, and his own network over a censorship problem. *This* confrontation resulted in his five week walk-out on the show and, ultimately, his resignation in 1962.

By the end of 1958, the program had more than surpassed the popularity of Steve Allen's "Tonight" and was on its way to becoming a legend in its own time. Viewing Jack Paar was like viewing tomorrow's headlines in the making.

Though he was often less than charming himself, Paar did attract a delightful array of guests to his show—several of whom appeared quite often. Among the favorites were Zsa Zsa Gabor, actress Peggy Cass, Cliff Arquette, writer and wit Alexander King, Pat Harrington, Jr. (doing his impersonation of Italian golf pro Guido Panzini), actor Hans Conreid, French singer Geneviève (who evoked laughs with her misuse of English), and the world's favorite hypochondriac, pianist Oscar Levant.

The public was divided on the subject of Jack Paar. People either loved him or hated him. But, they *watched* him . . . *talked about* him . . . and made him, undoubtedly, the most controversial television personality of his day.

Shortly after the unscheduled on-camera encounter between Griffin and Paar, the late night host ran into Merv's agent, Marty Kummer, and inquired as to the background of "that sharp emcee on 'Play Your Hunch.' "

"That's the guy I've been telling you about," beamed Marty.

Indeed, the MCA representative had, for some time, been after Paar to utilize Merv as a substitute host on

157

his highly-rated talk show, but had achieved no success. However, now that the star had witnessed Griffin's ad-lib talents for himself, he was more than willing to "give the kid a chance," and, within a very few days of their meeting, Merv got the long-awaited call to fill in for Jack.

Thinking that the uninitiated Merv would prove to be a total disaster in Paar's chair, Jack's first-line production team decided to take the night off (after all, who wants to be associated with a bomb) and gave the reins to aspiring producer Bob Shanks, a former actor and free lance writer, who was then a pre-show interviewer of guests for Paar.

Merv, although he'd waited for a golden opportunity like this for years, approached the actual experience with great apprehension. "After the first seven minutes on the air," he recalls, "I got up during the first commercial break and walked off in a panic. Bob Shanks stopped me and I muttered, 'I have to go home. I don't know how to do this.'

"He assured me that I was doing great, and, while Marty Kummer was backstage phoning all the network executives to watch me, I went out and, somehow, finished the ninety minutes."

So positive was the response to Merv's steering of the late night program, that he was called back twice during the next two weeks to repeat the chore: "The regular staff returned to work for my subsequent appearances, but I told them I'd rather have Shanks."

It wasn't long after Merv's repeated appearances on the show that Paar departed altogether. In an effort to find the right *permanent* replacement for the former host, the network began auditioning a number of performers in that slot . . . including Griffin, who did the assignment for two weeks.

On one of these shows, Merv's guests included wife

Julann (at one time considered by Paar as a replacement for his kookie Dody Goodman), the Smothers Brothers, and Hollywood's favorite butler, British-born character actor Arthur Treacher. A dapper and spry gentleman with an impeccable hauteur, the seventy-or-so-years-old Treacher had first met Griffin when he guested briefly on "Play Your Hunch."

Merv: "Tommy Smothers was going wild on the show, so I gave him the chair and, while he talked with Julann, I went over to the couch and chatted with Arthur. We got along beautifully and I told him that if I ever got a program like this of my own, I'd like him to be my sidekick."

Based on viewer and press response, as well as Merv's deft handling of the show, rumors began circulating that he would certainly be Paar's permanent replacement. Sadly, what he didn't realize was that, even as he did the late nighter, Johnny Carson had already been signed for the job.

NBC, though it had given "Tonight" to another, retained its interest in Griffin as the potential host of a similar program and, in July of 1962, decided that he would leave "Play That Hunch" (he was replaced by Gene Rayburn, and, later, his former boss, Robert Q. Lewis) to star in a fifty-five-minute daytime chat show, beginning in October. Said network Vice-President Mort Werner when he announced the new entry: "Merv Griffin is an entertainer of star magnitude. All those who have acclaimed his appearances on the 'Tonight' show know he has the ability to stimulate top performances by personalities in every walk of life. It is expected that Merv will draw heavily on his talent in planning his daytime shows. We know that his millions of fans are as delighted as we are over the bright promise of his new venture, which we intend to make amusing, adult, articulate and alive."

159

Griffin was overjoyed with the thought of having his own talk program, and had, in fact, initiated the idea at the network himself. Packaged by the newly-formed Merv Griffin Productions, the matinee music and chat show was pleasant fare, receiving fine reviews from the nation's television critics. *The New York Times* said the program provided "substance, glamour and fun in the afternoon," and, regarding the host himself, *Christian Science Monitor* wrote: "He is not forward; he does not sneer; he patiently aids his duller guests; and seldom misses an opportunity for humor."

Merv's producer on the show was Bob Shanks, the man who'd helped him through the Paar programs. Says Griffin: "I raised his salary from the two hundred per week he was making on the Paar show to a thousand a week on mine. I know I could have signed him for less, but I wanted him to have more than Carson's producer was making at that time. It was a matter of pride."

In a December 1962 interview with *The New York Times*, Merv said it was not his intention to give his show a daytime flavor: "I've noticed that there are just as many men as women in our studio audience. I've never directed the show to women. My wife taught me something about that. We'd go to parties sometimes where all the men would get together in one group and the women in another. Later, Julann would tell me she was dying to get over and hear what the men were talking about. I think a TV variety show should be for everybody."

Griffin was able to get many top guests on his afternoon program: Danny Kaye, Harry Belafonte, and newspaperwoman and author Adela Rogers St. Johns, among others.

Mrs. St. Johns: "I'd known Merv slightly when he was a little boy, since I used to play tennis with his Uncle Elmer, but I really got acquainted with him on this afternoon show. I did the first program and, also, the last. I was the unofficial pinch-hitter. Whenever a guest cancelled out, they'd call me because I lived only seven minutes away.

"Merv did some enchanting interviews on that show. He wasn't (and still isn't) afraid to ask questions."

Appearing with the outspoken Adela on the initial segment in the daily series was movie queen Joan Crawford, whom Merv asked: "Did you have any personal feelings toward any of the leading men you appeared with over the years?"

The actress replied in the negative, to which Adela answered, "Now, Joan, you married three of them. You must have had *some* feeling."

Over the years, Mrs. St. Johns has taken on a number of Merv's distinguished guests. She recently infuriated authoress Erica Jong by saying on the show that her bestselling book, *Fear of Flying*, was "too dull to read," and, prior to that, traded words with author Truman Capote. Asked if she'd read his *In Cold Blood*, the eighty-year-old journalist replied, "Why should I read a book about a page eighteen murder?"

According to Adela: "Merv loves it when I fight with the other guests. He eggs me on."

The afternoon "Merv Griffin Show" garnered a loyal audience following, but, regrettably, this was not enough, since the all-important Nielsen survey showed that its opposition, "Password," was winning the ratings race by a four-to-one margin. Network executives claimed the entertainment was just too sophisticated for the daytime timeslot and announced its cancellation effective April 1, 1963.

Adela Rogers St. Johns recalls that last distressing show. "Merv came out onto the darkened stage at the finale—carrying a suitcase, raincoat, and hat. He sat on the case and, with tears in his eyes, said, 'I'm so sorry. I just hate ending this show. Haven't we had a good time?'

"Then he sang 'Lost in the Stars.' It was very touching.

"He was so depressed. I don't think he really knew where he was going from there."

Hundreds of thousands of pieces of mail poured into NBC, protesting the cancellation of the afternoon talk show. ("It was the largest protest by viewers up to that time," says Merv.) Realizing that Griffin was a popular performer who might easily fit into another of their formats, the network attempted to sign him to an exclusive contract. Instead, he moved over to CBS-TV where he hosted "Talent Scouts," the summer replacement for "The Red Skelton Hour."

This entry afforded show business newcomers their first national exposure. Among Merv's discoveries while doing the short-lived program was comic Jackie Vernon.

Somewhat discouraged with networks, ratings, and the television rat race, Merv decided to try his hand in the often lucrative summer stock field and signed to star in two popular comedies, *The Moon is Blue* (at the Bucks County Playhouse in Pennsylvania) and *Come Blow Your Horn*, in Warren, Ohio.

The Neil Simon play was done for the Kenneley theaters, located in the mid-western states. ("I'd fly to New York every week to do 'Talent Scouts.' ") His co-star in that production was film star William Bendix, who, unknown to the rest of the company, was dying of cancer.

"Bendix and I clashed immediately," remembers Griffin. "I think he resented me because I was not a dramatic actor, but a television personality, and also because I got top billing.

"For the first few nights of the show, he deliberately

tried to throw me. He'd enter, go center stage, and, instead of delivering his lines to *me*, throw them out into the audience. Finally, after a couple of performances, I solved the problem. I walked right up to him and delivered my line right to his face.

"That was all it needed. He played it straight from then on."

From his experience with the now-defunct afternoon show, Merv had learned well that television is much more profitable when one packages (and, therefore, controls) a program, instead of just being paid a talent fee for his services. He also knew that, if he was ever again to have his own talk program (the only format he really wanted to do), he would, as before, have to create it himself. Consequently, he reactivated his Merv Griffin Productions, with the idea of packaging a number of television shows—one of which would, hopefully, be his own version of "Tonight."

Griffin brought his undying love for word games into play and created a show entitled "Word for Word," which was purchased by his old "friends," NBC. ("The network was desperate to get me back, so I said 'O.K., I'll go back—but only if it's on one of my shows.' It was blackmail, sure, but it made me feel damn happy.")

The game had contestants competing for prizes by trying to get the most three or four letter words out of a larger word. The winner would then try to unscramble a jumbled word and the number of such puzzles he solved determined how many prizes he won.

Debuting in early October of 1963, the daily show, hosted by Merv, did not receive good critical response. *Variety*: ". . . the show is quite average in format and, therefore, offers little to attract special attention. This, plus Griffin's mild, albeit polished, hosting, don't add up to enough excitement."

Merv's professional interests began taking up more

and more of his time and he found it was practical to spend weeknights at his Manhattan apartment, helicoptering home for Saturdays and Sundays (and every other chance he got) to see his family. Like other men who have successfully built business empires, the boyish-looking entertainer would find that, as the years progressed, he would be spending even less time at home, in order to meet the demands of the monster he had created.

It was Julann who came up with the basic idea for her husband's most successful television game show. "We were on a plane," she recalls, "on the way back from my home town. Merv was talking about game shows and, since that's all I'd heard him discuss lately, I said that I hated game shows. Then, just to be flip, I threw out, 'Why don't you give the contestants the answers, and let them come up with the questions.'

"Merv jumped on that idea and I realized that I'd thought of something good. He said, 'Give me some examples.'

" 'Five thousand two hundred and eighty.'

" 'How many feet in a mile?' he answered. 'Give me another.'

" 'Two-twenty-one-B Baker Street.'

" 'The residence of Sherlock Holmes.'

"Merv developed the idea from that point, called the show 'Jeopardy,' sold it to NBC (in early 1964), and, hosted by Art Fleming, it stayed on the air for eleven years, going off in 1974."

A man who keeps his promises, Griffin phoned his old San Mateo chum, Bob Murphy, when "Jeopardy" went on the air, offering him a job with his steadily growing organization. Murphy never had finished law school and was then selling real estate. He accepted the opportunity, moving back east to initially assume the function of selecting potential contestants for the new show. Murphy: "Merv upgrades everybody who works for him. He loves to see his people get ahead."

(Later, Murphy was promoted to associate producer when Merv began his next talk show in New York, and today is full producer of the Metromedia version of that format.)

Griffin has always enjoyed a close relationship with his employees ("I'm intensely loyal to my people and, in a dispute, I will take their word over that of the most prominent guest"). Julann, however, recalls an incident—when the packaging company was first created—in which certain of her husband's workers did *not* exhibit the same attributes: "I'd overheard two of the employees talking behind Merv's back, and I immediately tried to let him know who the disloyal parties were. But he wasn't interested. He said, 'Don't tell me. I don't care what they say as long as they're doing their jobs.'

"Merv has a remarkable ability to give people space."

During the first weeks "Jeopardy" was on the air, NBC's marketing department came to Merv to predict that the show would have a short life. What they said was needed were less intelligent questions asked of contestants. "I ignored their suggestions," reports Griffin, "and since the program had such a long run, I was, obviously, correct in my decision."

In less than a year, with two shows on the air, Merv Griffin had built his company to where it was one of the more sucessful in the competitive field of television packaging. But, still desiring a change of pace, he went back on the straw-hat circuit during the summer of 1964, for a nine-week tour (beginning in Bucks County) in a revival of the 1926 George Abbott-Philip Dunning play, *Broadway*. Appearing with him in the show, produced by his company, was Maureen Reynolds, the model on "Word for Word," and Julann's sister.

Aside from his business abilities ("I'm not a good businessman . . . I have good, astute people advising me"), Griffin was also garnering a reputation as one of show business' top all-around performers. In 1963, shortly before the Chief Executive's well-publicized trip to Ireland, he was invited to emcee the White House Correspondent's Dinner in Washington, D.C., for then-President Kennedy.

"Towering comedy writer Pat McCormick came to Washington with me to help prepare my monologue," remembers Merv. "I was petrified about doing this appearance, so, just before we went to the dinner, I asked Pat to take a walk with me. 'Pat,' I said, 'what happens if they don't laugh at the jokes?'

"He chuckled and replied, 'Tell them you'll reveal the name of the unknown soldier and blow the whole monument.' "

Merv, who had himself just returned with Julann from a vacation in Ireland, was to speak at this dinner—attended not only by the press corps, but also members of Congress, the Cabinet, the Supreme Court and the Diplomatic Corps. He had brought with him a performing company that included comedian Guy Marks, Edie Adams, and a new singer named Barbra Streisand.

The monologue went well, and Griffin ended it by relating an anecdote that he had debated excluding altogether:

"Mr. President," he began, "you're going to Ireland soon to see some of your relatives. Well, I've just returned from that beautiful country, and I had an experience there that concerns you.

"My wife and I were in a little town called Limerick, having a spot of ale in a local pub. A little old lady with a flowered hat came up to us and said, 'We know about you Americans with your riches . . . your refrigerators . . . your minks. We know how you get them.'

" 'How do we get them?' I asked.

" 'You charge them.'

"Then, she began talking about how you were coming to Ireland, Mr. President. She said, 'He's a good man . . . a good Catholic . . . and he's married to a fine, beautiful Irish colleen.'

" 'Excuse me, ma'am,' I interrupted. 'Mrs. Kennedy's maiden name is Bouvier. She's French.'

"That threw her for a moment, but she, finally, came back with, 'French, she is. Well I didn't think she was so much anyway.' "

President Kennedy loved the true story, and gave his permission for it to be printed in the nation's press. Usually, doings at these White House social gatherings remain off-the-record.

Merv was rather shocked that, after the performance when the entertainers went through the reception line to meet JFK, Miss Streisand, who'd received a tremendous ovation for her offbeat rendition of "Cry Me a River," had done the unforgiveable. She'd asked for an autograph.

"You shouldn't have done that, Barbra," Merv chided her at breakfast in the Washington Hotel next morning. "It was a dumb thing."

"I just wanted his autograph," she answered.

"What did he write?"

" 'Fuck you—the President!' " she replied, sending the table into hysterics.

Griffin, an avid nail-chewer, was somewhat amused when he met Kennedy face to face. "You know," he told friends later, "I looked at his hands and he bites his nails, too."

A few years later, Merv entertained at another White

House dinner—this one hosted by President Richard Nixon—and suffered a fate every performer dreads. "I had about ten powerful, topical jokes prepared," he recalls, still unable to accept the reality of what occurred, "and the speaker just before me on the bill did *nine* of them.

"I went out in front of that prestigious crowd and said, 'I don't know what to say to all of you. The first speaker did some of those stories better than I do them.'"

To an outsider looking in, it would seem that on New Year's Day of 1965, Merv Griffin should have been a contented man. Financially, he had security through his successful packaging company, and there appeared to be constant requests for his services as a game show emcee, as a guest vocalist on variety shows, and the like. About this time, he was also considering an offer to host a television program which would travel the globe, filming the world's top circus acts. He refused this job and subsequently it went to Don Ameche.

Yet, what Merv truly wanted was another shot at his own television talk show. The months he'd had the afternoon entry on NBC had been happy ones for the star, making him realize that he was most comfortable in that kind of format. So, he set about to find another home for "The Merv Griffin Show."

Group W—the Westinghouse Broadcasting Company—had previously had a certain amount of success with syndicated talkers hosted by Steve Allen and Mike Douglas. Now, they were seeking a new star for a ninety-minute chat show, which would be seen in five markets—Boston, Baltimore, Pittsburgh, Philadelphia, and San Francisco. If all went well, it would be sold across the United States and Canada.

Chet Collier, an executive at Group W, knew of Merv's talents in this area and was convinced he was the right man for the new slot. Once Griffin indicated he was amenable to doing a *syndicated* show, it didn't take Chet long to get his colleagues at the company to buy the entertainer's package, the deal being set in February of 1965.

The intimate Little Theater on 44th Street, next to Sardi's, was renovated to become the home of Merv's new show. Executive producer chores fell to Collier on this program (ultimately seen—mostly in daytime slots—in over one hundred and forty markets), with Bob Shanks holding down the producer's chair. Kirk Alexander directed.

When it came time to pick an announcer cum sidekick, Merv remembered his conversation on "The Jack Paar Show" three years earlier with Arthur Treacher. "I thought that an English-accented announcer and the age difference between us would be a rather fresh idea on this type of program," remembers Griffin, "but everybody else—including Julann—was against it. I was adamant in my choice, however, and Arthur was hired.

"At first, he really didn't understand this kind of show format. If I was talking with a guest who Arthur thought was a bore, right in the middle of the conversation, he would make some quite brutal asides to the audience. Sometimes it could be very embarrassing. I'd have to placate the guest with something like, 'Don't mind Arthur.'

"You might say that Arthur was the epitome of an English gentleman. He once told me his philosophy of acting: 'Say the words; get the money; and go home!' "

Debuting on May 10, 1965, with a guest list headed by Carol Channing, the five-times-per-week "Merv Griffin Show" received a mass of favorable notices from the critics. They not only praised the amusing chemistry between the star and his British cohort, but also were

169

impressed with the fact that, unlike rivals such as Johnny Carson, Griffin regularly brought on serious guests, furnishing his audiences food for thought, and, at the same time, provided the fun components expected on a program of this kind.

In a July 1965 interview with *The New York Times*, Merv said: "I long ago decided to be just Merv Griffin and let be what will. But I want this show to move out into the world, seek interesting people, explore ideas, find talents. If they can't come to us, we'll go to them."

And that's just what this charming host, with his refreshingly naive on-camera quality, did. Shows originated from such places as Monaco (with Princess Grace and Prince Rainier), in Cannes (featuring a singing Sean Connery), and from London (where Michael Chaplin knocked his legendary comedian father, and pacifist philosopher Lord Bertrand Russell discussed Britian's relationship with the United States, then attacked the Vietnam war). "We received criticism from all ends on that [London] one," says Merv. "New York papers attacked us by saying, 'It was a traitorous act for Merv Griffin to allow a man to come on the air and denounce the war.' "

Among the new talents Merv introduced on his show around this period were Reni Santoni, who later starred in the movie version of Carl Reiner's *Enter Laughing*; Richard Pryor; comic-actor Sandy Baron; singers John Denver and Lainie Kazan; funnyman Stanley Myron Handleman; comedienne Joanne Worley; Woody Allen; Tiny Tim; and future late-night rival, Dick Cavett, then a talk show writer who aspired to be a comedian.

Of course, once the word got out that Merv was giving breaks to untried talent, ingenious, albeit unknown, performers began breaking down the doors for an audition. Says Griffin: "One night my wife and I were leaving the studio to rush to a Broadway play. In the alley outside, there was a huge package addressed to me. The top of this great crate suddenly came off, and the sides fell down and there was a piano-player and a girl singer doing a number.

"Another time the elevator that led to my office opened—this was before we put a lock on the door—and a guy came in, didn't say a word, but began playing wooden flutes. When he finished, I said thanks and he left. Never did find out who he was."

Merv did well with the Westinghouse show, as he told Associated Press writer Cynthia Lowry late in 1966: "That's the beauty of syndication. If your show is broadcast by individual stations, instead of by a network, the local station managers decide where to put it, and what spot will be best for their audiences and, therefore, for you.

"We expected to be in the red for at least two years [the show, after eighteen months, was being broadcast by sixty-five stations, making it available to eighty-five percent of the nation's viewers], and so did Westinghouse, but we made it into the black much quicker."

Griffin, incidentally, who was once senior vice-president of the Catholic Actors Guild, was presented with that organization's Actor of the Year award about this time.

One of the Group W program's more interesting coups in the guest department was actor Marlon Brando, a personality whose television appearances have been virtually nil. The future Don Corleone was visiting his old friend Merv's office one afternoon, when the emcee suggested they pull a gag on producer Bob Shanks. "I took Marlon down to Bob's office," laughs Merv, "and introduced him as 'Bill Smith,' a new booker for the show. Bob was dumbfounded. He started to say that my companion looked just like you-know-who, when I interrupted him with, 'Don't start that shit about his being a double for Brando. Everybody says that to him.'

"We didn't prolong the charade very long, because I had to do the show. Marlon accompanied me to the theater, and it didn't take a lot of coaxing for me to get him to walk on stage. He stayed for an hour and was an excellent guest.

"Afterwards, I took him to Sardi's for dinner. He hadn't been there before. Walter Winchell and the opening night party of a new Broadway show came in. later and, since Brando's never out in public, they were shocked to see him. But, he was nice to everybody.

"We couldn't get a cab later, so we walked down Eighth Avenue. All the way, people were gawking at Marlon and we caused a tremendous traffic jam."

Merv was seldom without an interesting show and many of the Westinghouse entries were quite memorable. One, an hour special entitled "The Sidewalks of New York," was a musical salute to "Fun City," which received sterling notices from the critics. Highlights included Dionne Warwick singing at Central Park Lake and at the fountain in front of the Plaza Hotel; Dick Shawn and Renee Taylor doing a comedy sketch in Greenwich Village; Joel Grey singing "Give My Regards to Broadway" in Times Square; Hendra and Ullet performing a baseball satire in Shea Stadium; and Merv and Arthur doing such numbers as "New York, New York," and "Every Street's a Boulevard" in places like Rockefeller Center and on Park Avenue.

Ben Gross of the New York *Daily News* commented, "All in all a delightful divertissement that gave one a taste for more."

Another Griffin segment was called "Give a Damn" after Mayor Lindsay's campaign to better conditions and gain jobs for New York's ghetto dwellers. Guesting on that passionate, yet entertaining, plea to aid the poor, were Burt Lancaster, singer James Brown, Spanky and Our Gang, Gladys Knight and the Pips, and the one-and-only Muhammed Ali. The program was taped on the most desperate street in Harlem.

Almost nothing was out-of-bounds for Griffin on this highly rated nightly entertaiment. In December of 1965, he even took Treacher, his crew and guest stars (Carol Channing, Phyllis Diller, and Mahalia Jackson) back to his home town to tape a show in the College of San Mateo's Little Theater.

Certainly one of the most unforgettable incidents that ocurred during Merv's Westinghouse years was his feud with David Merrick. The renowned theatrical producer was an occasional guest on the show and had once walked off in a huff after trading words with comic Phil Foster.

"I received a tentative offer to play the Wednesday and Saturday matinees of Merrick's show, *I Do, I Do*," claims Merv, "but I was too busy and turned him down. I understand he got angry at my refusal and, for several months, we didn't exchange words, even though we were both always in Sardi's. It was rumored he told his actors they could not appear on the Merv Griffin Show."

"One night on my show, I decided to have some fun and announced to the world that Miss Miller, who was by now a regular with me, was going to be our Broadway critic. She would go to plays, then come back the next night and review them.

"Well, her first assignment was, naturally, a Merrick production that had received disastrous reviews out of town—*Keep It in the Family*. There was no way, I thought, that she could say anything nice about this play.

"Merrick was furious, incidentally, and said to the press that, by doing this, I showed a disrespect for the American theatre, and was trying to ruin Broadway.

"Miss Miller, accompanied by a member of my staff, went to the play—holding *paid* tickets—and, the next night, came back to the show to give her review. I had no idea what she was going to say.

"I introduced her and she announced, 'It's one of the loveliest shows I've ever seen.'

"I couldn't believe it. The gag had backfired on me, and Merrick seized the opportunity to tell reporters that Miss Miller was probably the most intelligent reviewer on the Broadway scene."

Griffin got the final laugh, however. *Keep It in the Family*, which opened at the Plymouth Theater on September 27, 1967, lasted a mere five performances. According to the papers, the flop dropped a ninety-thousand-dollar investment.

Merv took a fling as an investor in a Broadway show once: "The play was *You Know I Can't Hear You When the Water's Running*. I only read the first act, but it made me laugh so hard that I became a major stockholder. It was a big hit and, in fact, Marty Balsam won a Tony for his performance."

In 1968, Merv was back in Las Vegas (this time in the Riviera Hotel's Versailles Room) with a show that featured song-and-dance man Arthur Treacher, singer Gloria Loring, comic Marty Brill, and Griffin's own orchestra leader, Mort Lindsey. Said *Variety*: ". . . a strong package that is ideal nightclub fare . . . Griffin masterfully ties the party together, at one point singing quite effectively a medley of Bacharach numbers. His nostalgic piano salute to melodies made famous by ex-boss Freddy Martin brings warm applause; his 'Born Free' vocal accompanying himself at the piano is a zooming bowoff."

Merv returned to the motion picture screen in 1969. (He'd previously turned down important roles in Otto Preminger's *The Cardinal* and a Bob Hope comedy, *The Private Navy of Sgt. O'Farrell*.) The film was an amusing little Ivan Tors production for Paramount release, entitled *Hello, Down There*, which dealt with a family living in an underwater house off the Florida coast. Produced by George Sherman and directed by Jack Arnold from a script by John McGreevey and Frank Telford, the color comedy starred Tony Randall, Janet Leigh, Roddy McDowall, and, in a minor role, Richard (*Jaws*) Dreyfuss.

Griffin's function, originally conceived for Jackie Gleason, was to play himself . . . an easy task. He appeared briefely, supposedly interviewing the film's aqua family for his nationally-televised show. Of his contribution, *Variety* said: "Merv Griffin is in strictly for name value in his single sequence, but okay."

This was the performer's last movie appearance for a while. When we first went to press, Griffin had been signed to play himself in a suspense film from Universal, *Two-Minute Warning*. Larry Peerce directed the movie that starred Charlton Heston.]

Away from work, Merv was trying to spend as much time at his New Jersey home as possible, but a steady stream of commitments were making the weekend-only visits less frequent. Often, Arthur Treacher and his wife or other members of Merv's professional family would be invited to the farm on these days off. (Bob Murphy: "Even when Merv relaxes, his mind keeps working. He'd say, 'I can't wait for my vacation,' then, after a day on the farm, he'd be itching to go back to work.")

Julann, while her husband was away, enjoyed her role as a homemaker, especially in the baking of her own bread, fermenting her own wine, and coming up with a wide variety of unusual food concoctions. Keeping occupied like this made Merv's absences easier to bear. Many times, of course, the domestically-minded lady joined her mate in the city in order to attend some social function.

She helped Merv when she could and, in one instance, dyed his old tennis shoes black, so that he could wear them with his tuxedo. Since he detested his formal patent leather shoes, Griffin greatly appreciated his wife's gesture.

Like many of the New York-based television programs, "The Merv Griffin Show" had its own baseball team made up of staff members. Every Thursday they would play another show biz group in Central Park. "I used to pitch because it was my team," admits Merv, "but we were so bad that even the Playboy Bunnies beat us."

Summer, 1968. Merv Griffin had it all. His talk show was a winner; his packaging company was continually placing new game shows on the air ("Let's Play Post Office," "Reach for the Stars," "One in a Millon," "Talk It Up"), some of which were, however, short-lived; he had a special recording deal with MGM Records; a music publishing business; an independent movie company; close to two hundred people on his payroll. As he'd told an interviewer for *TV Guide* a couple of years earlier: "I've found what's important to me. At forty-one, I'm professionally and personally secure. What more can a man want?"

But, *was* he satisfied? As close friend and business associate Bob Murphy says, "Merv doesn't believe in playing things safe. He likes change."

CBS, about this time, was facing a late night crisis. Until now, the network had made no serious attempt to compete with Johnny Carson's "Tonight" show, leaving that time period for affiliate stations to fill. "We considered Carson almost impregnable," recalled

CBS vice-president Perry Lafferty to *TV Guide* in 1972. "He's the epitome of all that's attractive in a TV host—handsome, witty, fast and personable. For a while, our local stations were able to stay in the ball game with movies they had contracted for themselves. But, in the summer of 1968, they were running out of movies. Some of the films already had been aired five times. Our affiliates were being hurt in the ratings, so we felt the network had to move into late night programming."

The CBS executives considered several alternatives—everything from an updated version of the pioneer "Broadway Open House" starring either Dick Shawn or George Kirby, to late night soap operas. Yet, an informal straw vote from the network's affiliates showed that nearly eighty-five percent of these stations would prefer some sort of a talk show in that slot. The idea appeared workable to Lafferty and company, mainly because Joey Bishop's late evening chat program on ABC was making no significant dent in Carson's ratings. This meant that, in a three man race, the floundering Bishop would, more than likely, bring up the rear . . . making the real battle between Carson and the CBS host, *whoever* he might be.

That question was decided, almost immediately, when vice-president of programming Mike Dann received a call in June from the William Morris Agency, which was then representing Griffin. Remembering the succeeding chain of events in *TV Guide*, Dann said: "The agency asked if I were interested in Griffin for the late night slot. I said, 'Are you serious?' Griffin was then negotiating with Westinghouse for renewal of his contract, and nobody was sure how that would turn out.

"If Griffin did become available, the William Morris people said they'd need a quick answer from CBS. I promised them one and that was the end of the conversation."

When his agents informed Merv of their talk with Dann, he was not too enthusiastic about the proposal, but, after a bit of coaxing, acquiesced to his representatives' advice, informing them, "I want *double* the money Carson's making."

Aside from the vast amount of dollars involved in such a deal, as well as the prestige factor of being on a major network, there was, perhaps, a more personal reason for Merv's going along with the CBS idea. After all, wouldn't it be poetic justice if he could pull off a ratings victory over NBC . . . the same network that, a few years before, cancelled his much-loved afternoon talk shows?

Merv's handlers (specifically Sol Leon of William Morris and the star's attorney of long standing, Royal Blakeman) met with Dann and outlined the terms upon which Griffin would be willing to move to the network. The executive made some notes, then excused himself to go present the offer to his superior. A few minutes later, he was back, agreeing to meet all points in the proposal.

Dann: "Griffin's people looked at me in surprise and were shocked. They had come into my office at three o'clock and twenty minutes later had received a firm answer. They said they weren't prepared for that kind of speed and would have to go back and talk it over with Merv. I said fine; that night they called and said all was agreeable."

On August 6, *The New York Times* ran the announcement that Merv would be joining the CBS lineup in the Fall of 1969 (he still had to finish his contract with Westinghouse). Network president Thomas H. Dawson, counting on a one-million-per-week advertising gross from the entry, commented in the story: "We are convinced Merv Griffin guarantees us late night supremacy."

Asked what he thought of Merv's entering the competition, Johnny Carson replied: "I've had competition in the last twenty years. In TV you always have people opposite you. I don't know what it means. That's what I said when Joey went on the air."

Bishop, who had the only show of the three to originate from Hollywood as opposed to New York, was a bit more articulate: "The viewers are the ones to benefit from this. When you get competition, you work just a little harder. If you're the only craps player in town, you play the odds you want. Each one of us will be putting on our thinking caps as to how we can use our guests best."

Merv's deal with the network was an enviable one, giving him *total* creative control of his show. It also had the advantage—unlike the Group W program—of being topical. "The biggest drawback to the syndicated show," he explains, "was that it aired, in some areas, as much as five weeks after we'd taped it. We were always warning guests not to make any reference to dates or days, because they would be long past when people saw it.

"It was rough during 1968, the election year. And when Martin Luther King and Bobby Kennedy were assassinated, we had to just sit there as though it hadn't even happened."

The CBS show, on the other hand, would air later the same night it was taped.

Griffin, who'd enjoyed doing his Westinghouse program in the Little Theater next to Sardi's, nixed the idea of moving the show over to CBS's Studio 52 on the West Side Manhattan. ("It was right across the street from the lines outside the unemployment office. What could be more depressing?") He insisted that the network give him another theater from which to originate his interviews. After some banter back and forth ("I wrote my first letter of resignation"), the network agreed to convert the old Cort Theater, near Broadway, into a television studio. Total cost: two million dollars. ("Everything had to be perfect and comfortable. This was my five-hundred-seat security blanket.")

Built in 1912, the theater had housed many classic stage productions. Its opening play was *Peg O' My Heart* with Laurette Taylor. Indeed, some of the world's finest performers—Katharine Cornell, Fredric March, Basil Rathbone, Uta Hagen, Cornelia Otis Skinner, Katharine Hepburn, Lillian Gish, and Jose Ferrer—had trod the Cort boards.

As the debut date (August 18) approached, Griffin began giving publicity interviews on a marathon basis, in which he discussed programs like his: "They used to call talk show hosts traffic cops, but it's not all that easy. You have to put a framework around your guests. You have to lead them in the right direction. Meanwhile, we're all out in the open. You can't hide from the cameras. There's just one thing you can't have when you step out there—and that's fear.

"Jack Paar was the master of interesting small talk and he was also the master of the talk show interview. Politicians, incidentally, are very hard to interview unless you throw them a surprise question—but they've been tossed every question known to man. Athletes are pretty good, but raw and undisciplined.

"American actresses tend to be too leery; they hold back. But foreign girls are great—Sophia Loren, Lollobrigida, Cardinale, all fine talkers with a gift for candor. Except for Bob Goulet, who can be very funny, most singers are dull and they have no sense of humor about themselves.

"With three network talk shows now, it's going to be a battle for audiences. It'll also be a terrible battle for guests. Today the audiences have seen everybody, unless you can book Howard Hughes and Charles Lindbergh for the first show, which would be a great idea if we could pull it off."

Unfortunately, Merv was unable to get either Hughes or Lindbergh for his opener and, instead, had to settle for Woody Allen, Moms Mabley, Leslie Uggams, Hedy Lamarr, former presidential advisor Ted Sorenson, and, of course, second banana Arthur Treacher. (As with Treacher, Merv's former production staff —conductor Mort Lindsey, producer Bob Shanks, director Kirk Alexander, and chief writer Bob Howard—remained constant, as did the general setting for the interviews.)

"I walked out onto the stage," says Merv, recalling that first show, "and realized that, as a surprise, CBS had packed the first seven rows of the theater with fifty TV critics from all over the country. A hundred critical eyes staring up at me! I looked at them and went right into the toilet."

Most of the notices next day were mixed. David Elliott, writing for the *Chicago News*, commented: "It was a dull show, despite Arthur Treacher and his magisterial Bucks County walking stick. . . . Yet, the show was a success for Griffin, of and by Griffin. He appeared with all the efficiency, aplomb and casual charm he has shown the last four years on his syndicated (mostly daytime) program for Westinghouse."

For the first week his show was on the air, Griffin ran a close race with NBC competition in the Neilsen ratings, but the following seven days, he slipped well into second position with less than thirty percent of the audience. He remained there, except for an occasional instance when a substitute host was filling in for Carson, for the rest of the time he was on the network. Conversely, Joey Bishop trailed the field, ultimately being replaced on ABC by Dick Cavett.

As Merv, who stayed with CBS a total of thirty months, later told *TV Guide*: "It was in the second week of the show that I became convinced CBS already had given up on me. The pressures began. Little things. There was constant next-morning quarterbacking. There were suggestions that I bring in outside consultants. I was told to load the show with more guests—presumably so there would be less time for *me* to talk."

Weeks passed and Griffin, emotionally upset by the constant pressures from CBS, began to put on weight. ("I gained thirty-five pounds and ballooned up from 164 to 199 after I started the late night bit against Carson.")

Aside from the network conflict, Merv found himself faced with some difficult shows at the Cort.

In March of 1970, for example, CBS electronically blocked out almost forty minutes of guest Abbie Hoffman, a member of the Chicago Seven, who exposed to the cameras his red, white, and blue shirt. The network invoked the censorship because they felt this use of the American flag might be illegal in certain states.

"It was incredible," laughs Griffin. "It looked like I was talking to an empty chair. But the funniest thing turned out to be the Ford commercial CBS ran during the interview. It featured Roy Rogers and Dale Evans. They had on the exact shirt the censors decided was too unpatriotic for Hoffman to wear."

A few nights later, Merv decided to poke fun at CBS by blacking out his own opening monologue. As he explained to the audience what had happened to Hoffman, the entertainer was slowly cut off the program. At the end of the bit, he was down on his hands and knees, peeking through a small hole in the electronic curtain, declaring, "I have since talked with the president of the network and in the future such censorship editing of my show will not take place without my knowledge and consent."

After that, only his voice was heard: "Furthermore, it has just been agreed that I am to be the sole judge of censorship problems on my show if they should occur in the future. In this regard, CBS has decided to go along with my ultimatum.

"I don't like to swing my weight around like this, but as host of the show, I think I have some power (At this point, the whole screen went dark) to regulate and control what is to be shown and what isn't. That's all I have to say. May I have the network back, please?"

The following August, a group of sixty militant black musicians and other performers in the audience interrupted the talker by shouting demands for "equality for black artists," while playing their various instruments. Merv was forced to dismiss the house and cancel the taping. It was an unfortunate show for hijacking. Merv's guests that night were Dick Gregory and the ambassador of a new African nation.

With "The Tonight Show" so firmly entrenched as a national viewing habit for years, and the fact that CBS could only assemble 150 stations for their show, compared to Carson's 210 affiliates, it's no wonder that Merv had his rating problems. Things were so bleak that, by January of 1970, some committed stations had opted to running his show in the afternoons, instead of 11:30. The star's reaction: "It's silly for us to fight over sixes, sevens, eights, and nines, when there's an afternoon prime-time audience we could be playing to. People keep saying the prestige is in the late night spot. Yeah, King Constantine has prestige, but he hasn't got Greece."

Away from his show, good things seemed to be

happening to Merv. The New York Chapter of the National Academy of Television Arts and Sciences honored him at a dinner-dance, noting that he'd aided the careers of many entertainers by giving them an important television showcase for their talents; a new MGM record album, featuring the performer solely at the piano, was released; and he opened a restaurant.

Pips, as the eatery was called (after Arthur Treacher's nickname), opened on April 22, 1970 on West 48th Street beneath the offices of Griffin Productions, and had an Old English atmosphere. The host's partner in this establishment was veteran restaurateur Vincent Sardi, Jr. (Pips, sadly, was not to enjoy a long life. It folded after Griffin moved to Los Angeles.)

Merv was depressed. He'd come to the realization that his CBS talk show was in trouble rating-wise—bad trouble. He knew that, despite the large fee CBS would have to pay him for cancelling his non-option contract, he was dangerously close to losing the dream it had taken so many years to achieve.

"When I became aware the CBS show was failing," he remembers, "I knew I had to leave New York for a few days, so I could figure out what to do. I told Julann I'd call her and let her know where I was, then I drove to the airport.

"Almost in a daze, I flew to Los Angeles, hired a car, and went out to Malibu. I rented a house there for a month, then went to the supermarket and purchased a hundred dollars worth of food.

"The next morning, I woke up and said to myself, 'What am I doing? I can't stay here for a month.' I called some friends, told them they could take the house, then drove up to Carmel—still very confused.

"I walked around there for awhile, and, later, went to Santa Clara. Michael, my seventeen-year-old nephew (Barbara's boy), was in school. I picked him up and we

184

drove to Santa Cruz, all the time talking my problems out loud to him and then listening to Mike's problems. I ended up buying him a Volkswagen that day.

"Then, it hit me that I had to go home. I went to the airport and got on a plane. Just as they closed the door, the passenger next to me, a doctor, asked if I was okay. I spent the entire flight talking with him. That's really what I needed to do all along—talk my problems out loud to a professional man.

"When I got off the plane, everything was clear to me. I knew exactly the steps I had to take to save my show."

Merv had decided to move his show west to Hollywood. In the past, he'd originated the program from tinsel-town for a week or two at a stretch—to take advantage of the locally-based talent there—then followed this stint with a visit to Las Vegas, where he would tape some shows at Caesar's Palace. Each of these jaunts had produced an increase in ratings and, beginning September 9, 1970, the show would originate from Television City in Los Angeles on a permanent basis.

CBS may have been perturbed at Griffin's abandoning their two million dollar investment in the Cort Theater, but they had to agree with the star's reasoning: "It's terrible trying to get guests in New York. The worst problem is, naturally, that two other shows are on at the same time. There's a fourth show too—David Frost. He's syndicated and his time is different. But he still uses guests. Four shows tape every day with guests. Can you wonder they're hard to come by? Hollywood will give us a lot of fresh faces." (Also affecting the network's decision was the fact that a skyscraper under construction next to the Cort had caused one of the theater's walls to collapse.)

Duplication of guests on the quartet of shows was a regular headache on the New York scene. Jerry Lewis set some sort of a record in this area by appearing with Griffin, Cavett, and Carson—all in one evening. On another occasion, Hubert Humphrey was scheduled for Merv's show right after he completed a similar interview with David Frost. When the former Vice-President did not appear at the Cort on schedule, a Griffin staff member grabbed Humphrey by the arm, and led him off to his other engagement.

The migration to sunny, smog-filled Los Angeles resulted in some changes on the Griffin staff. Producer Bob Shanks and Arthur Treacher had both decided to remain in New York, the latter to oversee his chain of fish-and-chip eateries. (Treacher died in December 1975 at age eighty-one.) This meant there would no longer be a sidekick for Merv, and producing reins would now be assumed by the team of Saul Ilson and Ernest Chambers.

Merv moved the rest of his key staff members to the coast at his own expense, then set about to make his last ditch stand to rescue the network show.

His efforts were successful . . . temporarily.

Seven

When it came, the move to the West Coast was quite sudden, occurring over the long Labor Day weekend.

Deciding not to purchase a home until they got their bearings in this new environment, the Griffin family rented a large house on North Bedford Drive in Beverly Hills. "Almost immediately," reflects Merv, "the tourist buses were driving past the house and I was, frankly, quite surprised as to how quickly my new address had become public knowledge. But, as it turned out, *I* wasn't the attraction. It seems that I'd moved into a real tourist trap—the same house in which Lana Turner's daughter killed Johnny Stompanato.

"I always seem to move into houses with a sordid history. The next place we leased in Los Angeles was the old Lear/Firestone mansion. At one point, a potential kidnapper had been shot on the premises."

Julann: "It was a kick living in that huge Firestone mansion. The only problem was that things—plumbing, electrical—kept going wrong and we were always calling repairmen."

The advantage to living in California, where everything is "freeway close," was that Merv was now able to spend more time at home—physically, that is. On a mental level, he was often with his business interests.

The star arose every morning to play tennis and go for a swim. After that, he'd depart the household to take care of various matters, arriving at his CBS offices around four. His show taped from seven to eight-thirty in the evening, and he was usually home by nine-thirty for a light supper, then in bed long before his eleven-thirty airtime.

On weekends, when he wasn't required to work, Merv, Julann, and ten-year-old Tony drove down the coast to La Costa, near San Diego, where they sat in the sun, swam, and played tennis. Griffin became quite proficient at the sport, finding it very relaxing.

The one disadvantage in doing the show from the West Coast was that it was not seen until two days after it was taped. Oddly, two copies of the program were sent east for airing. Each was aboard a different jet flight—a precaution against hijacking. Quipped Merv: "Can you imagine what would happen if both planes were hijacked to Cuba? If he liked them, maybe Castro would request continued hijackings."

Griffin found that guest procurement was much easier in Los Angeles than it had been in New York. Regrettably, however, this availability of bigger name stars and Merv's innovative idea of doing shows with a single theme (i.e., Hollywood glamour, cooking, fat men, Hollywood tough guys, teenage alcoholism, etc.) didn't help the vital Neilsen ratings much. *They* did not increase, but the pressures on the host from CBS certainly did.

"I was nagged," he lamented to *TV Guide*, "about not having enough pro-Vietnam War guests; about the Gabor sisters' double entendres, and once a CBS executive physically tried to prevent Eva Gabor from walking out on stage until she pushed her bosom down. The network censors snipped whole sentences and paragraphs out of our tapes, making some of the conversation unintelligible. One executive snarled at me, 'No wonder you're doing so badly when you keep saluting shows like "All in the Family," which is going off the air.' That, of course, was before 'All in the

Family' caught on and shot up to number one in the ratings."

Merv and network program vice-president Fred Silverman began casting aspersions at each other. It started in the Fall of 1971 when the exec said in New York that he was considering dropping the Griffin show in favor of a format akin to the old "Broadway Open House." Said the VP: "The guy's in his second year and keeps losing stations."

Griffin retaliated with an announcement that he wanted a release from his contract, effective December 31 (the deal actually expired on February 15), then referred to the "funny little men at CBS" who hadn't promoted his show enough.

"I want to keep discovering new people," he told columnist Joyce Haber. "Silverman's favorite new CBS star, Sandy Duncan, first appeared on my Westinghouse TV show.

"As far as the ratings go, my show wins over Carson every night in L.A., and three or four nights a week in the seventy cities. This is all hindsight, but I should have realized it's very hard to work for a network that's never had a talk show. NBC is geared for that. It's had 'Today,' 'Tonight,' and Arlene Francis at noon. CBS is geared for entertainment."

Merv, when he'd requested his release, knew he had an ace in the hole. As far back as July, Al Krivin, the president of Metromedia (they'd previously done talkers with Donald O'Connor and Allen Ludden), told him that any time he tired of network broadcasting, he had a home at his old time period on Metromedia. It was a tempting offer—a relaxed show like the one he'd done for Westinghouse—and Griffin didn't want to turn the deal down.

Yet, with both CBS and their star wanting to terminate the relationship, there was still a major problem which prevented the break. With what was the network going to replace Griffin?

While CBS figured out a solution to its dilemma, Merv would just have to make the most of a bad situation.

Though its namesake remained in "bondage," Merv Griffin Productions (a non-public company) was still growing to the point where it had about three hundred seventy people on the payroll, grossing approximately $8.5 million in 1970. Among its assets were radio stations (today, they number seven), various television game shows, real estate (including a building in Rockefeller Center), and a firm called Racing Patrol, Inc., a closed-circuit TV system used at racetracks.

Merv, who has always had a very low tolerance for alcohol, finally gave it up altogether as a result of two shows he did at CBS: "One had a cooking theme, with guests like Vincent Price and Eva Gabor. We were sipping wine throughout and, by the final thirty minutes, I was totally bombed and acting very silly." (Reportedly, he spilled wine all over Eva's bosom.)

The other incident took place a few months later. "I'd been out having a drink with some friends before the show, and arrived at the studio drunk. The next day, CBS called and asked me to come over and view the tape. I couldn't believe the way I'd acted. At one point, I was singing and the microphone in my hand was up over my head.

"That particular program never aired, but it made me realize that I had to see a doctor to find out what my problem was.

"I had hypoglycemia—low blood sugar. Alcohol and several types of foods were out. I was forced to give up my two favorite things—wine and rocky road ice cream."

CBS, following a mass of rejections from stars like Bill Cosby, Sonny and Cher, and Rowan and Martin, finally decided to stick something "innovative" in their late night time slot. They purchased a package of old movies from MGM.

Merv was out—even though he was being forced to ride out his contract until February 15—and he was so delighted about it that he quipped to the trade papers: "I think the theme of my last show for CBS will be 'A Salute to Freddy Silverman—Ninety Minutes of Silence.' "

The thirty months of shows Merv did for the network, sadly, no longer exist. New York brass opted to erase all the tapes, believing that the raw stock was more valuable than the retention of the programs for their historical significance. ("Shows like our salute to all the great song writers were lost forever.")

The new "Merv Griffin Show," via Metromedia, was to originate from the old Hollywood Palace Theater, just north of the fabled intersection of Hollywood and Vine. Again, the star would have complete creative control and it was his plan to do a number of filmed programs, journeying to the out-of-town locations of various movies that were in production. In addition, a deal was set with the management of Caesar's Palace for several weeks of shows to be done each year from that fabulous Las Vegas hotel, utilizing performers who were then appearing at the desert resort.

A trimmer, happier Merv debuted his new talker—produced by Bob Murphy and directed by Dick Carson (Johnny's brother), with Mort Lindsey leading an eighteen-piece orchestra—on March 13, 1972. His guest list included Steve Lawrence, Dinah Shore, Dionne Warwicke, Milton Berle, Dom DeLuise, and Angie Dickinson. Commenting on the opener, Sue Cameron of the *Hollywood Reporter* said: "It is a comfortable show—Merv is easy to watch, and he has entertaining guests . . . Welcome home, Merv!"

Of the Metromedia environment, Merv himself would say to the *Associated Press*: "For the first time in my life there have been no major changes to make. Doing the show is a joy. The pressures are off. I'm more relaxed and the people around me are more relaxed.

"Syndication means an earlier hour in most cities and, for that reason, a larger audience. And it again gives us a chance to get out and discover new talent, which we did rather well in the old days.

"In a three-way competition, you don't dare put a new face on for fear the other guy will get Bob Hope. We never discovered anybody on the network because you couldn't take a chance. We were just so frantic and hectic."

Merv and his staff continued their policy (started at CBS) of devoting many of the Metromedia shows to a single theme. One ninety-minute segment, for example, was entitled "The Changing Church," and featured six religious figures as guests—three priests who had married and three who had stayed within the confines of church law. *Variety* termed the entry "absorbing."

An interesting program had to do with "Money and the Economy," and offered guests like C. V. Myers (of the *Meyers Newsletter*) and financial advisor Elliott Janeway. "I became angry with Janeway," recalls Merv, "when he got very pontifical and told me that unions run my show. *They* tell me what to do.

"I said, 'Mr. Janeway, all of a sudden you're an authority on television? Frankly, you're boring me to death. Why don't you stop giving opinions on an area that you really don't know anything about and answer the questions I've asked you.' "

Merv's jaunts to distant movie locales have been quite entertaining. A 1972 visit to the Stockton shooting site of Stanley Kramer's *Oklahoma Crude* resulted in a rare television interview appearance of star George C. Scott ("I was scared of *him*. His wife told me he was scared of *me*, or what I would ask him on camera."). Also seen were Faye Dunaway, John Mills, Jack Palance, producer/director Kramer, and Scott's wife, actress Trish Van Devere. Griffin's material was filmed over a three-day period outside the Northern California city.

Another special show was shot at the location of Metro's *The Man Who Loved Cat Dancing* in Gila Bend, Arizona—the same weekend that David Whiting, friend of the movie's star Sarah Miles, committed suicide ("I interviewed Sarah Miles before the tragedy and Burt Reynolds right after. The program added up to the strangest aura we've ever had on the air.")

Griffin's show was back in Northern California to visit the location of Paramount's "turkey," *The Klansman* starring Richard Burton. Merv obtained a good interview from the Welshman, but was unable to garner one from wife Elizabeth Taylor, who remained in Richard's trailer. It seems that the couple had been engaging in one of their frequent off-screen personal dramas and the lady was too upset to appear before the camera.

Never one to forget his home town, Merv even did a program in which he reminisced with Bob Murphy and Cal Tjader about their days in San Mateo.

Merv and his production staff were a little surprised to learn that the appearance of film stars on his program did not account for the largest viewing audience. "The shows that go right through the top in ratings," says the host, "are about health, that's Number One. Then beauty—particularly cosmetic surgery. And food. This is understandable. It goes straight to our most important viewers—women."

One familiar face on the Metromedia chat show is

Jack Sheldon, who Griffin describes as the "movies' version of a jazz musician," and columnist James Bacon tags "Merv's Phil Harris." A couple of times per week—when the trumpeter isn't playing a gig elsewhere—Griffin and Sheldon will trade remarks and, also, sing a duet together.

"I know that some of Jack's humor borders on questionable taste," confesses Merv, "but he always makes me scream with laughter."

The star recalls an incident that took place a few years back while his show was originating from New York: "Jack, Arthur Treacher, and I were doing a personal appearance in Atlanta at the Civic Auditorium. After the show, Jack took me down to the place where he'd started in the business—a strip joint.

"There we were . . . sitting in this place . . . smashed . . . acting very bad. Jack was yelling dirty words and I had a cigarette girl on my lap, while tourists snapped pictures of us. Suddenly, the tall, imposing figure of Arthur Treacher appeared at the entrance. He walked over to me, lifted the girl off my lap, and, very sternly, said, 'Young man, you have a very nice wife and son. I'd get my ass out of here if I were you.'

"He sent me home in a cab, then stayed there himself with Jack to have fun."

At the start of 1973, Griffin and MGM formed Griffin/MGM Records in a master purchase deal. First artists signed by the label included Kathy Carlson, Hedva and David, the group Junior Lace, and David Clayton Thomas. Merv's own recording of "Happy to Know You," which he'd debuted on the "Sonny and Cher Show," was the company's initial release.

Shortly thereafter, the entertainer received a special award from *Photoplay* "for his contributions to the industry as a multi-talented performer, captivating host, and devoted friend and patron of new talent."

February 7, 1973: The entertainment industry and the public as a whole were shocked to learn the Merv Griffins' fourteen-year marriage was over. Julann had filed for divorce.

Three months later, Merv discussed the split with columnist Dorothy Manners: "The break was the hardest thing Julann and I have ever gone through—or ever expect to. No one, not even our closest friends, knew we were having problems. The public did not know, but far more important, neither did Tony. We were painfully aware that we were breaking up at such an impressionable age in our son's life. We love him so much and he loves us."

To find the right way to inform his son of the unhappy situation, Merv sought advice from a psychologist, asking, "How do I get Tony through this?"

"My son was stunned when we told him," reflects Griffin. "His reaction was just what I'd expected—'Why are you doing this to me?'

"I just couldn't handle that and, as a result, got short-term professional help."

Unlike so many Hollywood marital breakups, the Griffins did not indulge in public name-calling. Each, in fact, fully understands why the relationship could not continue, and retains a high regard for the other, as well as a certain residual affection.

Essentially, what happened was that the couple "outgrew" each other. As Julann puts it: "I felt, like an old-fashioned wife, that the woman should support the man and forget about herself.

"With Merv, his work came first. A family tries to understand, but when does a family cease to be a family? He had a talk show five days a week and, when he got home, he was 'all talked out.' He didn't feel like communicating. I understood, but that wasn't the answer.

"We grew in different ways. I still love Merv. He's part of my family, but I'm not 'in love' with him.

"It was a valuable part of my life, but I'm growing now."

Merv tells a similar story about the split: "We developed in absolutely different directions. I went toward show business, whereas she wanted to explore and get involved in other areas that would benefit her . . . and suddenly, we realized that except for Tony, we no longer had much in common.

"Julann has incredible abilities. She borders on genius in her sense of humor and native intelligence. She should do something with her life and not just stay in the kitchen. She's too special a person for that.

"It's strange," muses Merv, "a lot of show business marriages that worked well in the east broke up when the couples moved to Los Angeles."

With Griffin and his companies worth many millions of dollars, it was not an easy task for him and Julann to arrive at a property settlement. Therefore, the divorce was not final until the early part of 1976.

Since he moved out of the family's newly purchased home off Mulholland Drive in Bel Air, Merv's town quarters are in a small cottage, formerly occupied by the late Susan Hayward, in the hills above Los Angeles' famed Sunset Strip. A nearby resident is director George Cukor.

However, every Thursday after he's taped his final show for the week, Merv flies in his Beachcraft Super 18 airplane up the California coast to his real home at Pebble Beach, on Carmel Bay. He has found peace in this quiet, yet luxurious, world, far away from the rigorous demands of the entertainment business, as have many of his famous neighbors (Clint Eastwood, Jane Wyman, Doug McClure, Jean Arthur and Kim Novak).

A frequent visitor to Griffin's retreat is his son, Tony, who accompanies his father there almost every weekend. In the three years since his parents' separation, the sixteen-year-old youth has adjusted well, remaining close to both Julann and Merv. Says his mother: "Tony is nuts about his Dad. I don't think he'll grow up to be a performer, but he just might make a sharp artist's manager some day."

Before he moved to Los Angeles, Merv had difficulty flying in a commercial aircraft, let alone a small private plane like the one he now owns.

"I was a white-knuckle flyer," he admits. "I was absolutely terrified when I stepped on a plane and would always ply myself with booze to build up my courage.

"When I first came to L.A. for CBS, I got so bombed that they had to practically carry me off the plane. The network execs must have wondered what they were getting into.

"I knew I had to beat this fear, so I decided to buy my own plane. Jacqueline Cochran, the well-known lady pilot, had her Beachcraft up for sale. That's the one I bought . . . with her pilot thrown in on the deal. But, I wouldn't get on it. I just let the plane sit out at Van Nuys airport for several weeks."

Finally, Merv realized that he was acting foolishly and one morning phoned his pilot, Crescent Clark, with instructions to meet him at the plane. "I want you to go up," he told Clark, "then land as soon as I tell you."

The flight lasted about five minutes. When they were on the ground again, Griffin asked his sympathetic employee to explain what all the dials on the control panel meant. "Which dials will fall if the plane's in trouble?" he wanted to know.

It took the star over two years, but, ultimately, he became comfortable flying with Clark. Later, Merv took lessons himself, so as to serve as co-pilot in his own plane and to solo in a single-engine craft.

Merv began to date on a fairly steady basis after his marital breakup, his two most frequent companions being Eva Gabor, also recently estranged from her spouse, and Carmel antique shop owner, Barbara Mac-Farland.

It was with Miss Gabor that Merv attended the Westwood premiere of *The Man Who Loved Cat Dancing*, doubling with the film's star, Burt Reynolds, and *his* then steady girl, Dinah Shore. Always a bit of the Irish rogue, our hero decided to play a little prank on Reynolds that night.

The movie was over and outside the theater a mob of cheering fans was waiting to greet their beautiful Burt and, hopefully, obtain a souvenir . . . an autograph . . . a button . . . shirtsleeve . . . a lock of hair. . . .

It certainly wasn't a confrontation that Reynolds was looking forward to.

"I'll get you out of here," offered good buddy Merv. "You go out the side door of the theater, and Clint and Maggie Eastwood, and Eva, and I will bring my car around and pick you up. The fans won't even know you're gone."

A grateful Burt agreed and, within a few minutes, the handsome actor was safely in the back seat of his friend's white vehicle.

Griffin, a wicked gleam in his eye, drove around the corner and stopped right in front of the theater. "Hey, folks," he yelled out the window, as he honked on the horn, "here's Burt Reynolds, Clint Eastwood, Dinah, etc."

Spotting this limousine of superstars, the crowd made a dash for it, only to be frustrated by the scampish driver, who zoomed away into the night.

Merv was vacationing with another lady friend in Hawaii a few months back, when he met, for the first time, two famous royal visitors: "The first morning I was there, I came downstairs in my shorts to play tennis and ran smack into Queen Elizabeth and Prince Philip, who were stopping in Honolulu, on their way to Guam."

Since his departure from CBS, Merv's professional life has enjoyed an ever-increasing upward momentum. Aiding in this success has been Murray Schwartz, once Griffin's agent at William Morris, but now the President of Merv Griffin Productions (the parent company of several corporate structures). This busy firm not only produces Merv's popular talker, but also "Wheel of Fortune," NBC's hit game show, as well as specials like "Take Me Home Again" with Burt Reynolds, "Isaac Hayes and the Stax-Memphis Sound," and "Paul Anka." Two seasonal shows under Schwartz's control are "Merv Griffin and the Christmas Kids" and "Merv Griffin and the Easter Kids." Both have featured some of Hollywood's most talented children—Rodney Allen Rippy, Ricky "The Partridge Family" Segall—cavorting with the host in musical numbers and skits.

Indeed, with its varied interests—both in and out of the field of television—the company grossed a record twelve million dollars in 1973.

Aside from his divorce that same year, Merv's company was served with a lawsuit—this one asking two hundred thousand dollars, and filed by Pamela Mason. The former wife of actor James Mason contended that she had agreed to do sixty-five one-hour radio shows for which she was to get one hundred dollars per show and one-third of all the profits from its syndication, which was to be handled by two firms owned by Merv.

The agreement was cancelled after Mrs. Mason did twenty-four shows, her legal representative said. Named as defendants besides Griffin and his companies was Caesar's Palace Hotel in Las Vegas, financier of the programs, according to the suit.

At this writing, the legal action is still pending.

Merv received further public flack when actor Al Pacino announced that, after doing the program, he'd sworn off on talk shows altogether because he felt Merv had asked him stupid questions. Griffin's reply through Dorothy Manners: "When Pacino started taking off on me, or the show, I thought he must have been on at a time when someone was subbing for me as host. I didn't even remember having him on. But we looked up the clips and, sure enough, it was me. It was a year or two before he broke big in *The Godfather*. He was appearing in some show on Broadway and neither was a hit. One of the 'stupid' questions I asked him was 'How did you make it from the Bronx to Broadway?' His bright answer was, 'By subway.' (This question, incidentally, gave us the idea for the fine, incisive TV series titled 'Take Me Home Again,' which we produce for syndication.)"

The year 1973 also found rival Johnny Carson abandoning his New York base and moving his highly successful "Tonight Show" out to the NBC studios in "beautiful downtown Burbank"—just over the hill from the Hollywood Palace. This change didn't bother Merv in the least, however. There were plenty of celebrity guests for everyone in Los Angeles and, besides that, the two programs were no longer competing with one another. Carson was still going on at 11:30, while Merv's syndicated show was seen around the country (in 122 markets) during afternoons and, in many cases, right in the middle of prime-time.

"Johnny doesn't do a rigid talk show," says Merv. "He puts on a bright, funny, show business get-together."

Griffin wasn't too well acquainted with Carson ("we did a panel show together a long time ago") when, a couple of years back, the NBC personality made a surprise appearance on his syndicated show: "I was introducing a new singer, whose first name just happened to be John also, and, to be cute, I said, 'And, here's Johnny!'

"Well, out walks Carson and the audience went wild. Dick Carson—*his* brother and *my* director—had set the gag up. It worked perfectly. He did an hour interview with me and it was a fun show."

In mid-July of 1974, Griffin was hospitalized with a mild case of viral pneumonia. Substituting for him on the show as guest hosts were Roger Miller, Helen Reddy, and Orson Bean.

The following October, Merv was honored when his name (the 1601st) became part of the Hollywood Walk of Fame—his star being placed in the sidewalk fronting the Hollywood Palace. Chamber of Commerce president Jerry Fairbanks and walk committee chairman William F. Hertz participated in the dedication ceremonies, which were videotaped as a special feature for the Metromedia show.

Merv received further laurels at the 1972-73 Emmy Awards where his program won three statuettes—Best Director, Best Writing, and Best Talk Show. Unfortunately, he lost the award for Best Emcee to Peter Marshall.

"It was the 'wives show' that won me my Emmy," explains Merv, referring to the memorable session that featured the spouses of famous men. "I think our divorce count is up to twelve—right off our marriage theme. Now, my whole orchestra wants to bring *their* wives on.''

He may not be on a network, but Merv Griffin—through his fascinating, thought-provoking, yet entertaining, interviews—more than likely draws a larger viewing audience (considering he hits prime-time in many areas) than any other talk show host including Carson. Comic Don Rickles gave a partial reason for his popularity during a recent visit to the program. ''Carson,'' Don said, ''tells the jokes; Mike Douglas—he's a kidder also, but, Merv, you're a *prober*, and that's what really makes an interesting show.''

Abe Vigoda (the late-blooming star of *The Godfather* and television's ''Barney Miller'') may have paid Griffin the ultimate compliment, however, when he told the host, ''My seventy-seven-year-old mother said her friends told her I was a movie star, but she didn't believe it for herself until she saw me on the 'Merv Griffin Show.' ''

Eight

Watching "The Merv Griffin Show," whether at home or in the studio audience, one could easily get the impression that staging this smoothly-run ninety minutes of entertainment is a relatively easy matter. After all, what's involved?

You rehearse a musical number or two, book a few guests, then sit around and chat. Nothing could be simpler.

Yet, present that hypothesis to a staff member over at Griffin Productions and you're going to get one hell of an argument.

Don Kane has been a talent coordinator with Merv's show ever since it moved from New York to Hollywood in 1970 and, prior to that, had held a similar position with Joey Bishop's late night talkathon. Although he readily admits that there is no scarcity of celebrities in the Los Angeles area who don't mind working for AFTRA scale, booking the program with the *right combination* of guests is often difficult. Indeed, there have been situations when—two hours before showtime—Don has pushed the panic button.

"The most frantic predicament we ever had," recalls Kane, "was the time we decided to devote a show to *Tarzan* and the actors who'd played him. Well, there were a lot of actors who'd done the role (like Bruce Bennett) who wouldn't come on, but we finally booked Buster Crabbe, Jock Mahoney, Ron Ely (the television *Tarzan*), and Jim Pierce, who'd played the part in silent films and had also married the daughter of Edgar Rice

Burroughs. We also set Johnny Weissmuller . . . at least we thought we did. He was in Florida and we sent him a plane ticket to get here. *That* was our mistake.

"The day of the show arrived, but Johnny wasn't in town. We called Florida and found out that he'd traded in his L.A. ticket for one to Acapulco—and had gone there on a fishing trip.

"I tried to reach him via the phone all afternoon and, finally, learned he was out on a boat. So, at five o'clock (two hours prior to taping) we had a meeting—Merv, Bob Murphy, myself, and the rest of the staff.

"We all agreed that it was ridiculous to do a show about *Tarzan* without Johnny Weissmuller. Still, four other guests were booked and we had to do something. Then, Merv, who was the calmest person in the room, suggested that we switch the theme to jungle and South Seas movies.

"I got on the phone and contacted Gardner McKay, who'd starred in a South Seas adventure series on television a few years back. He agreed to come down to the theater. After that, I called the South Seas, a Polynesian restaurant in town and at five-thirty—sight unseen—hired the entire floor show to come in and open our program.

"It was a pretty hairy evening, but the show turned out rather well."

Merv's programs fall in one of two different categories—theme shows and variety shows.

Programs devoted to a single theme originate either with staff interest in the topic itself or the availability of a particular guest who the producer or talent coordinators decide to build an entire show around. For example, if Billy Graham happens to be in town, the evangelist might provide the nucleus for a religious discussion, with three or four additional guests booked to complete the panel. The availability of Lili Palmer recently gave the talent people the idea of doing a program on "Hollywood Glamour," and Janet Leigh, Rhonda Fleming, and Ann Miller were set to appear with the former wife of Rex Harrison, who now resides in Switzerland with husband Carlos Thompson.

Every theme show *must* have one or two billboard names—celebrities who will attract viewers. A segment done on horror movies a few years back featured John Carradine, Glenn Strange (the last actor to play the Frankenstein monster at Universal), make-up artist Don Post, magazine editor/monster buff Forrest Ackerman, and Vincent Price—that particular program's drawing card. When the topic was the "Glorious MGM Musicals," guests included Howard Keel, Kathryn Grayson, Ann Miller, Fernando Lamas, and Donald O'Connor—all of whom are still easily recognized names.

One effective entry had no celebrities as guests, but, instead, utilized mothers of celebrities. Kane: "Unlike the rest of us, these mothers don't view their children as 'stars.' In fact, many of them were quite bitter about the relationship. We were getting comments like, 'He never calls me since he became famous.' It was a most illuminating discussion."

If a theme show does not concern the world of entertainment, then there must be at least one *nationally* known authority on the evening's roster. Programs on "Preventive Medicine" and "Famous Lawyers" headlined Dr. Linus Pauling and F. Lee Bailey respectively, whereas Elliott Janeway, as mentioned in the previous chapter, was the star guest when the subject was "Money."

A natural offshoot of the theme show is the "Salute," in which the entire program is designed to pay tribute to a well-known performer or film director. Again, the caliber of names available for such a show will be the final determining factor as to whether it will be scheduled in the first place.

"The program *must* have names of one sort or another," emphasizes Kane, "otherwise, we're not going to draw an audience."

When performer Tony Bennett was saluted, the show featured guests Peggy Lee, Fred Astaire, Johnny Mercer, Pearl Bailey, and Rosemary Clooney. On Lucille Ball's salute, the crazy redhead was joined by her husband, Gary Morton, and children (Lucie Arnaz and Desi Arnaz, Jr.), long-time co-star Gale Gordon, and surprise guest Bob Hope.

A tribute to director William Wellman (*Public Enemy, The Ox-Box Incident*) brought stars like Joel McCrea, Ida Lupino, and Mike Connors onto the program; and Bob Hope appeared again (this time with Bing Crosby and Dorothy Lamour) in a show honoring David Butler, who'd directed the trio—individually and together—on several occasions.

Perhaps the most sincere salute to a director was the one afforded the late George Marshall (*Destry Rides Again*). Kane remembers: "I was contacted by an agent friend of Marshall's who told me the director was attempting to get his autobiography published, but without success. He suggested that a Merv Griffin show devoted to him might help matters.

"A salute to Marshall could very well make a good segment, but everything depended on what stars he could bring with him. I was a little dubious because he was then semi-retired—only directing an occasional Lucille Ball show—and was no longer in a position where he could offer the guests a job. If they came on the show, it would be strictly out of friendship.

"I called Marshall, indicated our interest and, also, the requirements regarding guests. He understood, then said he'd get back to me. He did—less than three hours later—with commitments from Bob Hope, Lucille Ball, Glenn Ford, and Edgar Buchanan. The show was, of course, scheduled.

"The day before we taped, however, Marshall called and said that Hope had to cancel out due to a more pressing commitment. Therefore, would William Holden be an acceptable substitute?"

"My answer was, naturally, 'Yes' and Holden, who gained nothing for himself in doing the show, drove all the way up from Palm Springs to appear for Marshall. Now, that's really friendship."

There is no central topic in Merv's variety programs. These are, simply, straight off the cuff talk shows that will go in any direction the host or his guests want to turn the conversation. Nevertheless, as with the theme entries, they typically start with a desirable guest becoming available, then several varied, if complementary, personalities being found to fill out that particular ninety minutes. This was the way events developed in the recent show that featured Don Adams, Richard Castellano, Lynn Redgrave, and Henny Youngman.

"Don Adams called me personally," remembers Kane, "and asked to come on the program. He's a good guest . . . lively . . . has excellent anecdotes . . . and is not always available. In fact, the only time we get him is when he's promoting something, which, in this case, was his television show.

"Castellano had also been offered to us at that time. He, too, is a choice guest . . . . a completely different type from Adams . . . and their two names gave that particular program a strong audience appeal.

"Miss Redgrave had just come to town to do a play, and, whether she's a first-rate conversationalist or not, she has a good name for our purposes. A lot of times, we'll book somebody who, although they might not be the best on-camera guest, has a certain *curiosity* value that will attract viewers. The Redgraves aren't seen often on U.S. television—and, especially, not on talk programs. Happily, Lynn proved to be an *interesting* guest also.

"Henny Youngman comes to Los Angeles a few times each year and we always try to work him in. He's very funny."

Every taping has its headaches and a frequent one for the booking staff is the last minute cancellation. Perhaps the celebrity is ill, has been called out of town, or, in the case of television stars like Telly Savalas or Robert Blake, is scheduled for a night shooting. But, unless the absent guest is the pivotal element on that program—as was the situation with Johnny Weissmuller on the *Tarzan* show—there is seldom a need for alarm. Hollywood is full of stars. It's simply a matter of finding somebody available who doesn't mind doing Merv's show on short notice.

Certain personalities absolutely refuse to be an eleventh hour guest. Often it's a matter of ego that dictates this attitude ("If they really wanted me for the show, they should have phoned me earlier"). Whereas Kane can certainly understand this point of view, he explains that the replacement would never be invited if he wasn't really wanted on the program and, more than likely, was already under consideration for another show for which he would have received ample notice. Kane: "Many times it's the agent or publicist—and not the star—who gets uptight at our making such a late offer."

In any event, Kane and company always have a list of personalities who they know can be counted on in case of an emergency. It's not that these potential guests wait by the phone for a call, but, assuming they are free, each one enjoys doing the program; aways comes up with something entertaining to say; and has had enough talk show experience to know that cancellations do occur and there is no loss of face in being booked the afternoon of the taping.

This pinch-hitting list will vary from time to time, depending on how recently a particular name has appeared on the show. Some of the more current favorites include Zsa Zsa Gabor, Adrienne Barbeau, Hermione Baddeley, Richard Dawson, Orson Bean, and Milt Kamen.

Bob Murphy remembers a desperate night in New York when it wasn't enough to come up with a standby guest. He or she also had to be at the theater within ten minutes. "It happened while Merv was doing the show for Westinghouse. Since we'd been advised that the final two guests scheduled were en route, the go-ahead was given to start taping.

"Once the show had begun, however, I received two calls—one right after another. In the first instance, the guest was cancelling out because his father had just died and, in the other, the celebrity had suffered a heart attack. Within five minutes, our ninety-minute talk program had lost all but one guest.

"While my assistant got to Merv during a commercial break, I started making calls, trying to find a replacement who was only a block or two from the theater, and could be there *fast*.

"We were lucky. I found two possibilities at Sardi's and, after a little pleading on my part, they hurried over.

"Evenings like that are always amusing—*in retrospect*."

Aside from being an obvious substitute, the other hangup that will bother a personality is when he or she is scheduled as the final guest on the program. This is considered the least desirable spot because these guests are only on the air for fifteen minutes or less and many believe that the home audience will have virtually disappeared by the time they make their appearance.

This might well have been the situation when Merv aired opposite Johnny Carson a few years ago and viewers went to bed prior to the 1:00 A.M. sign-off, but such is not true now. Since moving to syndicated prime-time, ratings have shown that the program actually increases its audience as it progresses, with the highest numbers being present during the final half hour. Seemingly, people who become disenchanted with a network movie or dramatic show will switch over to Merv because it is a program they can get involved with. The final guest is, therefore, in a choice position from the standpoint of audience exposure.

Yet, despite these facts, celebrities remain petulant when assigned the caboose slot.

A good actor is not always an interesting talk show guest and can often be a rather dull conversationalist. For this reason, potential guests who are not *top* billboard names or lack the aforementioned curiosity value are usually interviewed by a Griffin staff member prior to being booked. Explains Kane: "Many times we find that these stars don't have the most exciting things to say, but we may use them anyway if they exhibit a lot of *energy*, which Merv can play off of. Guests like this can make the show fun, which is what we're out to accomplish."

Merv Griffin's policy is to divorce himself from the actual booking of his show. He leaves that task in the capable hands of Kane, associate producer Betty Bitterman, and producer Bob Murphy, who makes all final decisions in this area. Surprisingly, the host seldom knows who his guests are going to be until he arrives at the theater for taping. There, he looks over information sheets prepared by staff interviewers. These assistants have spoken to the celebrities that day to gather material from which Merv can formulate questions which will elicit the most amusing responses.

Unless he bumps into one by accident, the host does not see his guests until they walk on stage. That way, he is almost assured of a fresh confrontation. Merv: "Spontaneity is what keeps me, and the audience, from getting bored."

There are instances, of course, when Merv might have run into somebody at a party, then suggested to his staff that they book him in the near future. Conversely, if the host has been turned off by a particular guest on a program, he may indicate that it would be best if that personality was not used for awhile. Then, a couple of months might pass and his attitude will change. He'll indicate, "We haven't used so-and-so lately. Why don't we find a spot for him?"

Although there are celebrities who are currently on the "Don't Book" list for one reason or another, it's unlikely that any of them will remain there permanently. As with the wind, sentiments change and, on "The Merv Griffin Show," it's not difficult to get a second chance.

Virtually every one of Merv's shows contains some amusing or penetrating exchange between the host and his guests.

Richard Nixon, appearing on the program in 1968, while he was running for the Presidency, was challenged by producer David Susskind, another guest, who suggested that Democrats who voted for him in the 1960 election were religious bigots.

"While the next commercial was on," recalls Griffin, "Nixon walked off, and, the following day, Herb Klein, his communications director, called to ask us not to use the interview. I said, 'No dice,' but agreed to let him see the tape in advance of airing.

211

"Herb called me later and said it was the best interview his boss had ever given."

Sometimes Merv even shocks himself with his on-the-air queries. "We were doing a theme show on millionaires and I suddenly asked Del Webb if he was a Republican. He said he was, and I asked how much he gave to Mr. Nixon. Webb answered, 'One hundred thousand, and I'm sick about it.' "

The host's personal reaction to the now-former President: "Before I'd even finish a question, I could hear his mental filing cabinet click and a drawer slide open and a folder come out with the answer. Old darting-eye Dick. He looks here, he looks there, he looks here, but he never looks you in the eye."

Senator Thomas Eagleton had been booked on the show the same day the story broke about his history of mental breakdown. This revelation, as the world knows, ultimately resulted in the aspirant's stepping aside as the Democratic Vice-Presidential candidate in 1972.

Reflects the star: "Eagleton sent word asking if I was going to talk about 'it,' and I said, 'What are we going to discuss? Tap dancing?' Either we talked about the story or the interview was off."

Eagleton did the show.

Griffin tries never to exploit his own opinion on the program. "I bet to this day," he told *Newsday* in 1969, "my liberal viewers think I'm liberal and my conservative viewers think I'm conservative. Nobody knows for sure. My job is to get the best interview out of a guest, to find out what he'd about, to be an X-ray machine, to ask the kind of questions the audience would ask if they could get their hands on the guest. I'm a catalyst, a traffic cop. Sometimes I play confidant to my guest to draw him out. Sometimes I'm the devil's advocate. Sometimes I take him by surprise by being guileless, by asking him everything.

212

"Why, I asked Nelson Rockefeller something no one had ever asked him. I asked him how he made his first personal money. He was stunned. Had to think and then remembered it was by raising rabbits for Rockefeller Institute experiments."

Merv also threw guest Bobby Kennedy a curve when he asked him, "What was it your parents told you to get all of the Kennedys to devote their lives to public service?"

There was a long pause before Bobby replied: "Our father told us that this country had been very good to the Kennedys and that we'd damn well better put something back into it."

"Of all the poiliticians I've interviewed," reveals Merv, "I think only Rockefeller, Kennedy and Humphrey actually listened to my questions."

While he was with Group W, Griffin learned that former President Eisenhower was a fan of his show, so he flew down to Gettysburg to ask the general to let him film an entire program on his farm. Ike agreed on the spot, then said, "Let's talk about money."

"Fine," replied Merv. "What do you want?"

"Thirty thousand dollars."

Griffin said "Okay." ("What else do you say to a national hero and former President?") Unfortunately, the general suffered a heart attack shortly afterwards and the deal was never consummated.

Richard Nixon and David Merrick aren't the only guests to have departed Merv's show abruptly. Sardonic wit Henry Morgan made an unscheduled exit during a CBS taping in 1970. As he explained to the press later: "Merv was interviewing a blond actress, Louisa Moritz, and it was dreadful. He kept talking to her, but there was nothing coming back. Then Merv threw it to me. When you're doing a talk show and fighting a rating problem, you have a moral obligation to keep people from turning you off.

"I thought to myself, if I were home, looking at the set, that I wouldn't be watching this. I thought if there were people who were willing to watch it, then let them.

"The whole show was just dreadful and I couldn't see how it could help Merv in the ratings. I didn't leave funny or polite. I just left."

Merv is the first to admit that his disastrous interview with Peter O'Toole was really his own fault. He'd met the fine actor earlier in London. They'd gotten along well and, when O'Toole came to America a year later to promote *Lawrence of Arabia*, he agreed to do only one talk show—Merv's.

If the host had seen Peter prior to showtime, then there certainly would have been no problem, but, as things turned out, Griffin didn't recognize the tall blond stranger who walked on the stage after his introduction.

"*You're* not Peter O'Toole," said Merv with a gasp. "But . . . you've dyed your hair blond."

"Obviously," was the sharp, somewhat hurt, reply. "I *had* to dye my hair for the part in the film, and, now that it's opening, I wish to be recognized."

After they were seated, Griffin queried: "Is this your first trip to America?"

"Yes."

"Did you bring your family with you?"

"Yes."

Both Merv and the audience were well aware of what the star, angered by Griffin's less than flattering greeting, was up to. How can you conduct an interesting interview when the interviewee will only reply with one syllable answers?

Merv tried a different kind of question: "What are your hobbies?"

Absolute silence—except for a few giggles from the audience.

Finally, Merv decided that the joke had gone far enough. "Peter, would you like to leave now?" he asked.

"Yes."

"You'd love to go back to England?"

"Yes." With that, the actor called his host a "son-of-a-bitch" and walked off the stage.

Griffin also received a stony silence when, on another show, he made the mistake of surprising guest James Mason with: "You're such a nice guy, why does your ex-wife hate men so much?" It was an awkward situation, which Merv recovered from by asking the Englishman what his favorite film was. "When I have to resort to that," says Merv, "you know I'm defeated."

This exchange, incidentally, took place several years before Mrs. Mason filed her lawsuit against Griffin.

Former show producer Bob Shanks recalls an interview Merv taped in Paris with the great French clown, Fernandel. "There was a language problem, because Fernandel spoke very broken English."

"The French word for 'actor' is 'comedian,' so when Merv asked Fernandel who his favorite comedians were, the answer he got was 'Humphrey Bogart, Cary Grant. . .' "

"The Gabor sisters—Zsa Zsa, Eva, and Magda—did the show together once," remembers Merv, "and when I asked which one was the oldest, Zsa Zsa smiled and said, 'Mama.' "

Zsa Zsa, incidentally, made another appearance on the show, shortly after she'd been robbed of her jewels. Ironically, a fellow guest was ex-con and onetime safecracker, Willie Sutton.

"On another program," says Griffin, "Don Rickles was bragging that he was such a big hit in Las Vegas that a hotel had named a sandwich after him. Phyllis Diller quipped, 'It must have been a *tongue* sandwich.'

"Once Rudy Vallee told me that credit cards had brought him and his wife closer together. 'I never let her out of my sight when she has them,' he said."

"The Duke and I—Merv Visits John Wayne," was the title of a January 1971 entry on the CBS program. Griffin and his crew had filmed the show the previous Thanksgiving Day weekend at Wayne's twenty-two-thousand-acre ranch near Phoenix. Between clips from the star's films, Duke told anecdotes, made political observations ("I felt so kindly this year, I sent Senator Fulbright a turkey full-dressed, but I couldn't resist telling him what he could do with it!"), and discussed his image ("I've killed so many Indians on the screen. Jane Fonda sends me hate mail").

Said Tony Scott in a *Variety* review: "Griffin's visit to Wayne was an absorbing portrait of an actor unafraid to express opinion."

An earlier program featuring love goddess Rita Hayworth did not go as well for Griffin. Critics found the conversation rather dull, citing that Merv did not probe deep enough, or, perhaps, Miss Hayworth was unwilling to be too candid about her personal life.

"Did you find Orson Welles overwhelming?" he asked the star at one point.

"No," she replied. "But I think he found *me* overwhelming."

When he inquired as to whether she remembered meeting him at a Jack Warner party some years before, she said cryptically: "No."

Sonny Tufts presented an interesting challenge to the host when he came onto the stage, obviously under the influence of alcohol. Remembers Griffin: "Nice to see you, Sonny,' I said as he came out. He looked at me and said, 'Boola, Boola.'

"What did you say?' I asked him. 'Boola, Boola,' he

216

said again. For twenty minutes, he answered every question with 'Boola, Boola.' ''

There was a time when a Mr. Fuchida, one of the planners of the Pearl Harbor attack, was a guest. ''The studio audience gasped when I introduced him,'' reflects Merv. ''But, after he had finished, this former enemy, whose ambition was to teach Christianity in California, was greeted with loud applause.''

Recently, Merv introduced actor Earl Holliman as the only TV cop (''Police Woman'') whose sidekick (Angie Dickinson) wears a bullet-proof vest by Maidenform.

''And a Cross-Your-Heart shoulder holster,'' retorted Earl.

One of Merv's earliest theme shows was a salute to comic strip character Charlie Brown on his twentieth birthday. Guests included ''Peanuts'' creator Charles Schultz, film and television producer Lee Mendelson, animator Bill Melendez, and spunky actress Karen Valentine, who, with Schultz, reenacted some Lucy and Charlie Brown encounters.

In 1971, while he was at CBS, Griffin conceived the idea of doing a show about nudity. Two naked people would be on stage—the cameras showing their faces, but focusing on audience reactions. Network censor Bill Tankersley, unfortunately, quashed that idea: ''There will be no nudes on CBS premises.''

Merv attempted to do a similarly themed program at Metromedia, but was politely asked to abandon it. Considering his good working relationship with the syndication company, he agreed.

Griffin, like any other talk show host, has had his share of censorship problems, primarily because a guest has made a slanderous statement or used a four-letter word on the air.

''Jackie (Moms) Mabley was frequently on my show,'' explains Merv, ''but all you ever saw were her lips moving. Practically everything had to be bleeped out. But people loved her.

"She was really something," he continues. "She would arrive in a chauffeur driven car, dressed to the hilt, with a fur stole around her neck. Then downstairs she goes to change. Off go the fancy clothes, out come the teeth, and she's ready to walk on stage."

Gypsy Rose Lee pulled a stunt on the old Westinghouse show that the home audiences never got to see. "The orchestra was playing a strip number," chuckles Griffin, "and Gypsy got up there and started swinging. Then something must have clicked. She turned her back to the audience and down went her pants."

The host still cringes when he relates what happened in his interview with British actor Emlyn Williams: " 'How does it feel to be the king of the English Theatre?" I asked him. And he replied with a profanity.

"I asked him a second question and he gave me the same answer. Then on the third query he almost shocked me off the show. His lips started to form a word that would need censoring after the censors got through. Knowing he had me on a spot, he changed it in mid-stream, thank God."

Over the years, a dazzling and varied array of guests have appeared with Merv—everyone from show business personalities like Helen Hayes, Red Skelton (an entire show was devoted to this great clown), Groucho Marx, and Danny Thomas to political and reform leaders like Mrs. Martin Luther King, Miss Angie Brooks (President of the UN General Assembly), and Congressman Adam Clayton Powell to sports figures Joe Namath and New York Mets centerfielder Tommie Agree. These and other notables have, indeed, provided us with thousands of hours of stimulating, candid conversation—brought about, for the most part, by Merv's ability to gain his guests' confidence.

Playwright Edward Albee was enjoying some light

exchanges with the host when Merv suddenly asked him what he thought about the performances of Elizabeth Taylor and Richard Burton in the movie version of *Who's Afraid of Virginia Woolf?* Although slightly startled by the suddenness of the query, Albee felt secure enough with Griffin to launch into an interesting comparison between the stage and film portrayals.

Along this same line, Mary Livingstone Benny, extremely shy regarding public appearances, told Merv in an interview: "You're the most relaxing person I've ever worked with."

"A Salute to the Silents" was a warm, nostalgic theme program, which featured eighteen of the screen's earliest players as well as clips from their pictures. On the program were Lillian Gish, Richard Arlen, Laura LaPlante, Viola Dana, Neil Hamilton, Jackie Cooper, Betty Bronson, Chester Conklin, and Ken Maynard, among others.

Former cowboy star Maynard appeared on the program slightly inebriated and, in the middle of his interview, made a quick exit—nature having called—by forcing open an electronically-controlled door, located center stage. Elderly Betty Blythe (*Queen of Sheba*) caused other problems. Recalls Don Kane: "She really didn't know where she was. We decided it would be kinder to edit the tape during her interview."

Said the *Hollywood Reporter*: ". . . as with the best evenings of any talk show, one wouldn't have minded if this one had lasted far into the night."

Going back to his younger days in the entertainment business, Merv devoted two entire shows to saluting the Big Band era, with guests that included Lawrence Welk, Bob Crosby, Horace Heidt, Les Brown, Vaughn Monroe, Connie Haines, Charlie Barnett, and, naturally, Freddy Martin. When it was Martin's turn to conduct, Griffin couldn't resist the temptation of joining his former boss on the bandstand to sing his earlier hits, "I've Got a Lovely Bunch of Coconuts" and "Wilhelmina."

"We had Eddie Albert and Eva Gabor on the program one night while they were starring in 'Green Acres,' " remembers Merv. "Television critic Cleveland Amory, who'd recently panned their show, was also on . . . and *that* was something.

"Well, Eddie and Eva waited, then both of them let Amory have it. They sailed into him. Actors can never forget a bad review!"

Don Kane: "Merv has been responsible for a lot of performers getting their big breaks. Tony Orlando and Dawn snagged their own series after they'd done our show, as did Sonny and Cher. George Carlin, Jose Felicciano, Richard Pryor, Rip Taylor, and Lily Tomlin all received their first important exposure through Merv."

"I recall the shock registered when Tiny Tim was first on the show," says Griffin. "It was the only time in my years at Westinghouse that our judgment in booking talent was questioned. We assured our critics that Tiny Tim was what was happening in New York at the time, and you can see for yourself what happened to him after that appearance.

"Dick Cavett's debut was also something a little different. Dick had been a writer for another late night show, but wanted to go it as a comedian. He couldn't get a spot on his show, so he quit one Friday and the following Monday made his first professional appearance with us."

Randolph Churchill's guesting back in 1966 resulted in a tricky exchange. After the Englishman was seated, he bluntly inquired, "I say, am I being paid for this?"

Merv answered in the positive. He was receiving the fantastic sum of $265, which was then AFTRA minimum. Churchill haughtily replied that he'd got two thousand dollars for doing a similar program.

"Only two thousand?" countered Griffin with a mock look of surprise. "You really were underpaid, because they usually pay seventy-five hundred for a guest like you."

February 1970 found Merv and a skeleton crew flying up to San Francisco to film a show on Alcatraz. This was the first time an entertainment type group had been permitted on "the Rock" since it was taken over by a group of about one hundred Indians two months earlier.

"Just setting foot on the historic island was an experience in itself," recalls Merv. "Seeing what the Indians had done there and feeling the aura of brotherhood that prevailed throughout the entire new community really left me breathless."

Surely the most frightening experience Griffin has had on his program occurred fairly recently during one of the company's regular jaunts to Caesar's Palace in Las Vegas.

A wild animal act had just finished on the large stage and, while the trainers were leading their unpredictable charges off, a large Bengal tiger, frightened by a camera hood, bolted and ran out onto a ramp leading to the audience. It was a tense few minutes—with the scared beast about two feet away from the closest members of the petrified spectators and ready to spring at any moment.

If anyone was the hero of the moment, it was Merv, who, while the trainers tried to collar the animal, moved to the edge of the stage in an effort to calm his audience. ("What else could I do? If anyone had panicked and ran, that tiger might have sprung at them. Besides, my 'buddies' in the orchestra had left the stage and *locked* themselves in *my* dressing room.")

The excitement was over within five minutes and, fortunately, there was no damage or injury . . . except to the program itself. The video recorder had run out of tape just after the incident had begun.

Being a talk show host can, indeed, be a hazardous profession.

Epilogue

"I'm really terribly shy," confesses Merv Griffin. "Walking into a restaurant full of people or, during the first half hour at a party, I'm extremely nervous . . . and I've been fighting this fear all my life."

Certainly this is a surpising revelation from such a clever, outgoing man, who has, for years, worked in front of live audiences and appeared perfectly relaxed.

"The odd thing is that I have absolutely no fears about my own show," continues the star, "because, there, I have my own people around and I feel comfortable with them. If a substitute cameraman is on one night, it, frankly, jars me.

"I'm not like other hosts. Jack Paar, for example, worked off a level of hositlity; Carson's bag is aloofness; I work closely with the people who work for me—my professional family. But, while the show's taping, I won't let them act as stooges, standing around laughing at the jokes. In fact, there's a rule: no friends or family or staff in the first six rows of the theater."

The only time Merv has been uneasy in doing his program is when he was not properly prepared—a situation which occurs *very* seldom. He, as might be expected, insists that his employees be as well primed as he in their individual tasks. "I've only seen Merv angry when somebody didn't do their job properly," reports a staff member. "His is not a violent anger, however. He smolders, becoming cold and biting, and refers to the object of his displeasure as 'Pal.'

"If a guest on the show gets out of line with a remark,

Merv will 'kill that person with kindness.' Somebody like Carson, on the other hand, would turn on that guest and make him look foolish."

Bob Murphy: "I've never seen Merv thrown. There have, of course, been hostile guests on the show, but he either wins them over or ignores them. On a few occasions when a guest has become too nasty to him, the studio audience—always in Merv's corner—has responded by, simply, turning-off on that personality."

Merv's entire personnel is devoted to him, as he is to them. ("Even when I've been cancelled, I've never laid off my basic staff.") He pays them well—much better than the "Tonight" show—and, as one top employee puts it, "He has an enormous enthusiasm for whatever he does, which is infectious."

Griffin is a rare man who never forgets a friend. Johnny Cochran, who worked as a sideman when Merv was with Freddy Martin, has appeared on the show a few times, playing in the orchestra when Martin was guesting: "Merv's always found time to break away from what he was doing and spend a few minutes chatting with me about the old days and what I was doing now. Every time I've done his program, he's seen that I've gotten extensive camera coverage."

Jean Barry Plant, Martin's former secretary, still sees Griffin often, and recalls that, thirteen years ago—on the eve of her wedding—she received a call from Merv, who was then living in New York: "He wanted me to come there and work for him. I said I was getting married the next day, and he replied, 'Aw, Jean, do you *have* to?'

"He was only kidding, of course, and when my husband, Harold, and I went to New York on our honeymoon, he showed us a grand time."

Irving Taylor, producer of the old "Hazel Bishop Show," hadn't seen Merv for nearly a decade when, a couple of years ago, he underwent heart surgery. The day after the operation, Griffin sent a huge vase of flowers to the songwriter's hospital room.

Merv's reluctance to burden friends with his personal problems, especially since his marital split, has provided the otherwise open performer with a few desolate hours. "It's tough when the curtain comes down at the end of a show. Ninety minutes of probing, intimate conversation stops, and the other people go home to their families or on to their outside lives. It can be lonesome, at times."

Although he has no immediate plans in this area, he would like to marry again someday. "I'm pro-marriage. I have to be married. I must have that one-to-one relationship."

Apart from his renewed interest in tennis ("I've become a real tournament player"), the biggest influence in Merv's personal life since splitting with Julann has been his discovery of TM (Transcendental Meditation), the Indian form of mental discipline that has attracted the Beatles, Clint Eastwood, Joe Namath, Efrem Zimbalist, Peggy Lee, and thousands of other followers.

"Clint Eastwood got me into it," remembers Griffin. "We both live up in Pebble Beach and when I used to phone him in the morning to set a tennis match, the maid, who didn't speak English very well, would answer and say, 'I sorry. Mr. and Mrs. Eastwood doing their BM.'

"I thought it rather funny that the maid would reveal such personal information, so I mentioned this to Clint afer it happened a few more times.

"He, of course, explained that she was referring to TM—transcendental meditation—and how the thing worked. Frankly, I thought it sounded freaky, until he said that, when directing a movie, he could set an entire scene in meditation, then come out and shoot it immediately.

"Well, my marriage was breaking up, my thinking was scrambled, so I asked Clint to set me up with a teacher—and the results were instant.

"Within a month, my stress left me . . . my mind became more orderly. Now, I meditate twenty minutes in the morning and twenty minutes at night, and just this amount of time makes me alert mentally and fit physically. It has helped me immeasurably in my work on television; I think I am a better questioner, and I respond more quickly."

Merv devoted an entire show to TM—his principal guest being the movement's leader, Maharishi Mahesh Yogi. ("The program was the greatest impetus given the movement in the United States. A month after we've aired, TM had forty thousand new followers.")

If and when he has time, Merv is a reader ("I'd take Charles Dickens, Edgar Allan Poe, and Victor Hugo to a desert island with me"), listens to classical music ("Chopin, Grieg, and Tchaikovsky are my favorites"), argues religion ("I'm a Catholic—I fight with other Catholics"), and expounds on his heroes ("I admire most of all the powerful, romantic figures who put this country together, men like Thomas Jefferson and Patrick Henry").

He doesn't really like to attend Hollywood parties, because he finds the typical chit-chat that goes on at such affairs inane and dull. ("I flee from boredom.") Merv, however, will attempt to liven up a tedious party—once he feels comfortable in his surroundings—by going to the piano and leading a sing-along.

Nevertheless, the peacefulness of his Pebble Beach home is much more desirable to him than these social gatherings. "I've got the greatest shut-off valve in the world," he says. "When I leave Los Angeles, I don't like to discuss show business. I don't even want to think about work.''

This is certainly a major change in a man who, only a few short years ago, ''thrived'' on his professional activity. Score one for TM.

Nor does Griffin like to make any long-range plans anymore. Though he is always developing new projects, like a mail-order business to promote the work of Monterey Bay artisans, he really prefers to take things day to day.

An eternal dieter with (according to Don Rickles) three sets of clothing, Merv is well contented with the life he has achieved for himself—by himself. (''If I could live my life over again, I wouldn't change a thing.'') It was, indeed, a difficult struggle at times, but this goal-oriented performer always knew that he would make it; it would simply be a matter of time.

Unpretentious almost to a fault, he does not even today consider *himself* to be a star. As Julann puts it: ''Merv is still in awe of people—even those he doesn't like—who have the talent to make it to celebrity status.''

Adela Rogers St. Johns considers Griffin to be ''an important influence in this country. He's as well-liked as anyone else we have.''

There's certainly no question about the truth of this knowledgeable lady's observation. Anybody who regularly reaches as large an audience as Merv's has got to be a significant force. With his show recently renewed by Metromedia*, he is likely to retain his ascendancy for many more years to come.

Merv Griffin—''a hip choir boy,'' ''a sophisticated wit,'' ''the total man,'' but, also, one hell of a nice guy.

---

*Since January 1976, ''The Merv Griffin Show'' has been headquartered two and one half blocks south of the Hollywood Palace, on Vine in the plush TAV Studios.

MERV: *Four Years Later*

Author James Michener guested on Merv's show awhile back and, during the course of the interview, remarked: "Talent isn't rare, but *disciplined* talent is very rare."

"I believe that wholly," Merv told writer Don Freeman in a *Saturday Evening Post* story (October 1979). "The stage is my home. I'm showbusiness trained. If there's one quality that I'm proud of (and it's so necessary), it's discipline. I'm disciplined as a performer.

"I'm always in control. If I see a guest falling apart, maybe fumbling on an anecdote, I can step in with a line. There's only one thing you can't have when you walk out there in front of the camera—and that's fear."

With his syndicated talk show currently being seen on 115 television stations in the United States and Canada, it's apparent that Merv's discipline continues to serve him well. His keen perception allows him to gauge his guests; to sense any anxieties; then to help them to feel more secure in front of the studio audience. One of his techniques is to interview a nervous guest *standing* out on center stage.

"I see what you did," Dustin Hoffman told Griffin after a show. "I get it. The big problem is fear of an audience. So what you do is, you bring the guest down to the audience right away."

Indeed, Merv will keep a nervous guest close to the audience until the fear has been conquered. On some nights, he's had to literally hold onto the performer until the fear disappeared from his eyes. Then, they sat down and continued with the interview.

Such consideration for stars unaccustomed to working regularly in a talk/variety format continues to ensure Merv a constant flow of top talent and hard-to-book guests. One of his favorite interviews in recent years was with former 1940s movie queen, Gene Tierney. "That forty-five minute interview," he said, "confirmed my belief that the talk show is at its best when there's reality at its core."

Laura was perhaps Tierney's greatest film, and it also happens to be Merv's favorite. Prior to introducing the actress, he sat down at the piano and played the movie's classic title song to set the mood. "Gene had been be-deviled by problems," recalled Griffin. "It was a dreadful life for a woman who was once a major Hollywood actress, and she talked about it with candor and honesty. It was for me and I think for the studio audience and the viewers, unforgettable."

In early April of 1979, the International Ballroom of the Beverly Hilton Hotel was transformed into the old Coconut Grove, with Freddy Martin's orchestra recreating the sounds of that era. The black-tie, star-studded occasion was to honor Merv, who that night was presented with the Will Rogers Memorial Award by the Beverly Hills Chamber of Commerce.

Orson Wells gave an eloquent tribute, magnifying the honor. "The talk show is *the* TV art form that is unique to TV," said Welles. "It was never as good on the radio. It obviously couldn't happen in the theater or anywhere else. It is pure television form. There are a few talk show giants. I'm here to salute my favorite.

"A good host must be considerate to his guests, and bring out their best. Merv's enthusiasm is genuine. . .a real actor is a re-actor—he knows how to genuinely listen. They tell me he's very rich and he deserves to be. He's very rich in friends and I am proud to be one of them.

"To be able to genuinely listen in front of all those millions of people, to bring out the best in people without endlessly trying to score off them, or to be funny . . . to be compassionate, to be amusing and amused, to be concerned and intelligently concerned—all these are the definition of the classic talk show host and the best of all talk show hosts."

"Orson Welles makes you feel immortal," responded Merv when he came to the podium. "I didn't know I was that great." Then, with Martin's orchestra playing "I've Got a Lovely Bunch of Coconuts" as background, Merv recalled the days when he sang with Freddy at the old Grove—twenty-seven years before. A few minutes later, he was singing the old songs, like "Tonight We Love," while everyone danced. It was a truly memorable night.

Another fun-filled evening for Merv occurred when he returned to San Mateo High School for a class reunion. Serving as emcee of the alumni show in the school auditorium, he faced his former classmates and announced, "Some of you here tonight may not remember what I looked like when we were in school together. So, to refresh your memory, I'd like you to meet a carbon copy of the way I was—my son, Tony!"

At that point, Tony Griffin, who was seventeen at the time and 6'2" and very slim, walked onto the stage. "The place went wild," recalled Merv. "There were great howls of laughter, especially from those who remembered how portly I looked when I was Tony's age."

Tony, incidentally, has grown into a young man of whom his parents can be justly proud. He attended Palos Verdes' Marymount College, then the College of the Seven Seas and was in the first group of students to enter Red China. Although he resides with his mother, the youth is following in his dad's footsteps. He studies telecommunications and heads a musical group called Karma Rock.

"Tony worked for his father," says Julann Griffin. "He started as a gofer on such shows as 'Dance Fever,' then decided he should go back to school. He realized that show business *is a business*, so he's taking business courses."

The former Mrs. Merv Griffin is also pleased with her life today. In 1976, she, with nine other ladies, founded the First Women's Bank of California, located in Brentwood. She remains on the board of directors of that institution, which has assets of over ten million dollars, and also goes out and addresses business groups on its behalf. One would think that this plus the time she spends overseeing the management of her four east coast radio stations (granted to her in the divorce settlement) would keep Julann very busy. It does, but now she plans to get into performing. Steve Martin has asked the former comedienne to appear on his next television special for NBC. "I'm getting out my old tap shoes," she says.

As always, Julann remains on friendly terms with her former husband.

And at this writing, Merv is also single—with no known plans to change his status. As he told the press: "I don't want to get married at the moment."

There is no indecision when it comes to Merv's professional life. During the past four years, it has had only one direction—upward.

In 1979, he was seen as himself (interviewing Alan Alda) in Universal's acclaimed feature film, *The Seduction of Joe Tynan*. Barbara Harris, Meryl Streep and Melvyn Douglas co-starred with Alda in this project, which Alda also wrote and which was directed by Jerry Schatzberg.

Television, nevertheless, remains Merv's stronghold. His production company keeps busy, doing shows like "Dance Fever," which features a disco beat. The star maintains a healthy creative interest in these other programs, although the actual day-to-day producing is left to others. Griffin still puts the bulk of his energy into his own talk show.

November of 1979 found Merv taping his 2000th program for Metromedia. The special show was staged at New York's Lincoln Center. The host, amid hundreds of fans, cut a huge cake and received the center's Commemorative Art Medal for his "love and affection for the performing arts."

To compete with the other talk/variety shows on the tube, Merv continues to tape his programs in places other than Los Angeles. He's in Las Vegas eight weeks of the year, drawing on that town's huge reservoir of talent. Atlantic City, Venice, Monaco, Egypt and Israel are just a few of the other locales he's visited since *Merv* was first published.

While doing the show in Monaco, Griffin visited one of the local discos and observed that the dancing was less frenetic there than in the United States. "Our clientele," explained a waiter, "do not care to perspire in their Dior gowns."

Christmas 1976: Merv's show originated from the Holy Land, retracing the life of Jesus. Locales included the Mount of Olives, Bethlehem and the Basilica of the Nativity, Jordan, Cana, and Capernaum. Archbishop Fulton J. Sheen, opera star Richard Fredericks and Father Godfrey of the Franciscan order in Israel guested.

While he was filming in Tel Aviv, Merv had the honor and the thrill to appear as guest conductor for the

107-piece Israeli Symphony Orchestra—performing his own contemporary concerto, "Monterey" in the Mann Auditorium. (He'd previously debuted the piece while guest-conducting for the San Francisco Symphony.) Merv accepted his baton from Zubin Mehta, who was conducting for the Israeli Symphony.

"Conducting a symphony orchestra is the realization of a lifelong dream for me," said Griffin. "In rehearsal, I just picked up a baton and started. The first couple of times the orchestra screamed with laughter—I lost them all—and I just held my head in my hands and they fell down screaming."

Mehta had cautioned Merv that the Israeli musicians might not know him. Being serious artists, they seldom watched the mass audience shows on television. "So there we were in the middle of rehearsal," recalled Merv, "and the trumpets were just having a terrible time with one passage which was a highly screaming, almost Stan Kenton jazz thing. I asked the translator to ask them if I could change that line to help them at all, and one of them stood up and, just clear as a bell, asked, 'Where is Jack Sheldon?' "

Extremely pleased with his musical endeavors, Merv comments: "They constitute a very gratifying personal forte, and I plan to pursue them increasingly."

Theme shows continue to be a regular feature on "The Merv Griffin Show." Among some of the more recent topics covered were "Transexuals," "Governors," "Children of the Rich and Famous," "Prisons and Prison Life," "The Polish Show," and "Pet Adoptions," featuring a rare television appearance by Doris Day. Merv also does entire programs built around the opening of a new movie, such as his recent tribute to the Kirk Douglas/Martin Sheen/Katharine Ross film, *The Final Countdown*.

Of course, from a different standpoint, the most

memorable shows are those in which something went wrong, like the time Sammy Davis, Jr. was doing a song and got mowed over from behind by the motorized bandstand. Then, there was the kid performing in a salute to amateur talent, who got scared and threw up on the piano.

These shows, however, are much more fun to remember than to experience.

Trumpet player Jack Sheldon and Mrs. Miller have been familiar faces with Merv for years. But, relatively recently, the public became acquainted with Vincent Montone, an usher at the studios where the show is taped. Indeed, Vince is probably the most famous usher in the country. Every so often, Merv calls him up on stage to do impressions of celebrities like Fred MacMurray and Paul Williams, or, with Montone in the audience, the two will trade wisecracks back-and-forth.

As a show biz sage once said, "Talent is everywhere."

A frequent visitor to the show, Robert "Baretta" Blake, who is known for his searing honesty, once told the press: "The nicest thing that I can say about Merv is that he's still on the air. That's not only nice for the American people, it's also vital. Without shows like Merv's—and certainly his is one of the best—there would be no place for the people of America, be they celebrities or otherwise, to talk to the people of America.

"God help us if the AMA, the PTA, the DAR, or the Ku Klux Klan decides tomorrow that talk shows are injurious to our children's brains. If they do, I'll be happy to stand by his side and put those scoundrels in their place.

"I wish him a long life and a continued very long and very successful career. I need him, and so do you."

Bob Hope is another who is not shy when it comes to

234

praising Griffin: "Merv is one of the clever landlords of 'plug alley,'" the comedian told the *Hollywood Reporter* in a 1977 issue honoring Griffin. "He is a man that not only knows his craft well, but knows yours and what you are selling. So, if you need anything, see Merv, not for money but for help. He's a delightful guy."

Comedienne Phyllis Diller: "He plays great tennis, great piano and conducts a great interview. He's a gentleman and a scholar and he ain't so bad in the accounting department, either.

"Once when I was in New York on Thanksgiving Day, he invited me to dinner at his home so I wouldn't be lonely. That's wonderfulness personified, because he knows I'm a sloppy eater. I adore Merv and have since the day I met him. We are born under the same sign, in case it comes up at a party, Cancer."

Commenting in the same *Hollywood Reporter* special issue, Paul Williams said of Merv: "A very nice guy, very stable. For him life is easy. Personally, I think Jack Sheldon is the one who should be honored. He's in full boogie orbit night and day, and he's never even seen a spaceship. He doesn't need one!!!"

Finally, comedian David Brenner believes that Merv's success is proof positive "that a nice guy can win."

So it goes. The compliments never seem to end. Everybody loves Merv—the celebrities, the audiences, the public at large.

He's a nice man. That doesn't change.

And, since he's recently signed a new deal with Metromedia, we are assured of his continued presence in our homes for years to come.

It's comforting to know that our old friend is going to be around.

Afterword

Merv was very pleased with this book when it was first published in 1976.

He told me so in a letter in which he jokingly suggested that, should I ever sell the movie rights, Robert Redford was his choice to play him.

It's not too often that the subject of an unauthorized biography will cooperate with the writer. And, with the current vogue of biographies that scandalize the dead (Tyrone Power, Errol Flynn, Joan Crawford, etc.), any future cooperation from the show business community is going to be even more difficult to obtain.

I was lucky. Merv graciously gave permission for his family, staff, and friends to work with me, then himself provided many hours of in-depth interviews. He did not insist on copy approval—only the right to read the manuscript and correct errors of fact. Not surprisingly, he utilized this privilege quite sparingly, merely changing a name or date here and there, or embellishing an anecdote. Opinions and value judgments by myself and others were not touched.

Not only did Merv plug the book innumerable times on his show, but he also invited me to sit on the panel one night. That was quite an opportunity. It gave me the chance to actually experience something that previously I'd only observed.

Doing publicity is nothing new to me. Indeed, it's my profession. I get a kick out of chatting about Hollywood nostalgia or related topics on radio talk shows. It's fun.

Appearing on local television interview programs in a one-to-one discussion with the host is also easy, though I do tend to be a bit self-conscious. The television camera adds weight. Certainly I'm no Orson Welles, but then my physique doesn't rival Pat Paulsen's either. Still, with an intelligent host, these shows are also enjoyable.

"The Merv Griffin Show" was a different case altogether. I don't mind admitting that the thought of being seen nationwide by millions of people was inhibiting—even for somebody as glib as myself. It was almost frightening.

Family, friends, business associates, potential clients, and old school chums would be watching me —wondering if I would make a total ass of myself.

And, to make things worse, I wouldn't be up there with easygoing Merv alone. I'd be surrounded by some very clever people—all professional entertainers. I prayed they wouldn't book Don Rickles that night.

Talent coordinator Don Kane phoned me around noon on the fateful day. "Tonight's the night," he said. "Be here at six. You got the author's spot." (Authors are brought on talk shows during the final fifteen-minute segment.)

I was almost afraid to ask the next question. "Who are the other guests?"

"Mel Tillis, Robert Clary, and Milt Kamen."

I breathed a sigh of relief. I'd interviewed Bob Clary for the book. A week before, I'd met Tillis when he and one of my publicity clients had appeared together on the "Dinah Shore Show." We'd had a friendly chat. And, although I'd never met Milt Kamen, I knew he was a gentle man—unlike some comics.

I went home early that day, called a friend and asked her to accompany me to the studio. Then, I showered, changed clothes and spent several hours pacing my living room, trying to think of clever things to say on the air.

We arrived at the studio fifteen minutes early. I continued pacing in the green room—until one of the production assistants arrived to greet me. Then, I became "Mr. Cool" (on the outside). I, after all, knew these people from my frequent visits there with clients. Letting them see me on the verge of nervous hysteria certainly would not enhance my image as a calm, level-headed publicist.

"How about a drink?" asked the assistant, as I signed the show's liability release form. Wisely, I opted for a Coke. I didn't want to relax too much.

The other guests wandered in one-by-one, with entourages of various sizes trailing along behind. Tillis and Clary knew me, of course, sensed my anxiety, and tried to make me feel at ease. Kamen was also friendly. He was curious about how I'd researched Merv's biography. "I've thought about doing a book," he said. "Maybe we could talk sometime." (Kamen died about three months later.)

The taping began. People in the green room stopped chatting and focused their attention on the monitor. Merv, wearing a rather subdued sports coat, open shirt and sweater, entered to huge applause. He began announcing the evening's guests. "Biographies of show business personalities are very popular today with the book buying public," he said, coming to the end of the line-up. "And there's a new one just published about one of the most fascinating, magnetic, and charming performers around today. It's called *Merv*."

Big laugh from the audience.

"The author," he continued, "is a Hollywood publicist, and has written other books, such as biographies of Paul Muni and Basil Rathbone. . . ." A worried expression crossed Merv's face. He turned to someone off-camera and said: "They're both dead."

Another laugh from the crowd. Merv concluded my introduction by quoting from a very favorable review of the book, recently published in the *Hollywood Reporter*.

I was summoned to the make-up room. While pancake make-up was being applied, the production assistant gave me a list of questions that Merv might ask me on the air. Such a gesture was not the program's usual practice. I guess that Merv okayed it because he knew I was a virgin and needed an edge.

As the moment of my appearance grew closer, my palms began to sweat—profusely. My gut became tight. I continually checked to see that my fly was zipped.

"Michael Druxman, on stage," bellowed the voice over the green room speaker. The assistant led me to the stage. I'd been there many times, but tonight he felt a need to lead me.

I honestly don't remember that much about the interview. Somehow I managed to walk out onto the stage, go through the usual handshaking, and sit down. Merv asked me about writing the book. I got him to relate the Errol Flynn story (see Chapter One). The other guests were very gracious.

One cute thing happened at the end of the show, which, because we were running late, never got on the air. Bob Clary tossed the book to Kamen, who threw it to Tillis, who tossed it back to Clary. Merv, in a mock panic, exclaimed: "Stop! That's my life you're throwing around."

The show aired a month later. Suddenly, I became personally aware of the power of television. During the week after the telecast, three perfect strangers approached me and asked, "Weren't you on with Merv the other night?"

That was four years ago. I still see Merv whenever I'm

down at the show with a client. Always warm, he refers to me as "my biographer."

Merv recently came out with his own autobiography. If you've enjoyed this book, why not pick up a copy of his.

Michael B. Druxman
July 29, 1980